Zuniga, Martinez de

An historical view of the Philippine Islands

Vol. 1

Zuniga, Martinez de

An historical view of the Philippine Islands

Vol. 1

Inktank publishing, 2018

www.inktank-publishing.com

ISBN/EAN: 9783747780978

AN

HISTORICAL VIEW

OF THE

PHILIPPINE ISLANDS:

EXHIBITING

THEIR DISCQVERY, POPULATION, LANGUAGE, GOVERNMENT, MANNERS, CUSTOMS, PRODUCTIONS AND COMMERCE.

FROM THE SPANISH OF

MARTINEZ DE ZUÑIGA.

PUBLISHED AT MANILA, 1803.

IN TWO VOLUMES.

WITH

A NEW AND ACCURATE MAP OF THE ISLANDS,

FROM THE BEST AUTHORITIES, PUBLIC AND PRIVATE.

TRANSLATED

BY JOHN MAVER, ESQ,

VOL. I.

LONDON:

PRINTED FOR J. ASPERNE, CORNHILL; AND NONAVILLE AND FELL, NEW BOND-STREET:

By T. Davison, Whitefriars.

1814.

INTRODUCTION.

The original, of which the following translation is offered to the English reader, is, probably, the only copy which has yet reached this country. Whether the chance which threw it in the way of the translator may be deemed fortunate or otherwise must be left to the decision of the candid public; but it appeared to him that the information it contains respecting a Spanish colony, the most interesting of any other to a British subject, supplies that desideratum so much wanted in our language;—*a correct view down to a very late period of the Spanish establishments in the Philippines.*

The position of these islands, and, indeed, that of the eastern Archipelago generally, whether considered in a political or commercial point of view, is sufficiently important. They form the entrepôt of Europe, India, China, the immensely extended regions of Spanish America, the north-western coasts of the new, and north-eastern coasts of the old world; and in the storms which at present convulse the political atmosphere of Europe, as well as that of both the Americas, it is not easy even to conjecture what may be their fate.

The productions of these islands are various, and of a value and importance unquestionably high. In the hands of an industrious population, and under a fostering government, there is scarcely any vegetable substance which, by slender exertion, they may not be made to yield, whilst the choicest treasures of the mineral kingdom, lodged beneath their irregular surface, minister largely to the cupidity, and furnish materials for the more enterprising labours of man.

Gold is in abundance; iron, steel, copper, lead, pitch and tar, hemp, cotton, indigo, sugar, cocoa, pepper, betel, cowries, tortoiseshell, mother of pearl and pearls, hides, coyar, tobacco, corn and rice excellent and abundant, with a variety of other productions, contribute to the wants of commerce; while in this enumeration will be found all the articles which, with the aid of the finest building timber in the world, are requisite for the construction and complete equipment of ships of every description.

The established intercourse of these islands with Japan and China offers a ready transit for manufactures; and although it is understood that the East India Company furnishes an adequate supply of our woollen staple to the China market, we may yet fairly expect that British enterprize will not overlook the advantages which the opening of the India trade holds out in this quarter; nor will the introduction of British manufactures into these islands, either with an ultimate view to the above markets, or to those of Spanish America, in any material degree interfere with the staple trade of the Company: there is full scope for adventure in this new vineyard, and labourers will not be wanting.

The political jealousy, and the national and religious prejudices of the Spaniards, have till lately opposed a bar to an extended intercourse with the Philippines; but the tide which hitherto has flowed in that direction seems of late to have commenced its ebb. The events of thelast twenty years have been in their nature so extraordinary, and in their effects so powerful a solvent of all the prejudices, fostered by ignorance and superstition, that the dawn of a new day seems to open upon mankind, Let us hope that while these clouds vanish before the morning sun, the great bonds of society will remain unbroken, and that the liberties of Europe, and consequently those of the world, will be fixed on a permanent foundation.

amelioration, have been suffered to make under the Spanish monarchy during the period in question. At any rate, we have grounds for supposing that if any alteration, favourable or unfavourable, has taken place, Zuñiga has contrived to weave it into the work; for it is asserted by those whose residence renders them competent judges, that the view he gives of the settlement is correct to the latest period.

The origin and language of these islanders have engaged the attention of our ablest orientalists. From certain similar characteristics in the persons of the inhabitants of the interior, or aborigines of the islands, they have hitherto had an African origin assigned to them; and nearly from the same source (Madagascar), it has been supposed that the Malay population has flowed, which has in a great measure inundated the Archipelago, as well as some parts of the continental coasts.

Similarity, or even approximation of language and manners unquestionably offer great facilities in enquiries of this nature, and they have accordingly been resorted to by all our oriental physiologists in their researches respecting the eastern Archipelago; and so far as regards the Malays and Malayan language, these researches have been attended with corresponding success; but in respect to the aboriginal language, or

Tagalic, very slight attempts have been made to trace it beyond the quarter in which it was found to prevail. Our author has not failed to enter into the discussion, and from the premises he lays down, not unreasonably, draws the conclusion that the Tagalic language and original population of all the islands westward of the coast of South America derive from that continent.

It is certainly consonant to reason to presume that the aborigines, or mountaineers of the interior of these islands, in their primitive state, were more likely to change their residence (if intentionally) by committing themselves to a favourable breeze blowing pretty constantly in one direction from the eastward; or if in consequence of misfortune, by finding their efforts unavailing to encounter an adverse wind, and again reach their own coasts; than to suppose even with all the aid the monsoons could afford them in an erratic navigation from Africa through the Indian ocean to the Archipelago, that they should diffuse themselves from that point in every direction over the South Sea, in the face of an almost constant current of wind, blowing occasionally with extreme violence.

The Malay population most probably had its origin as stated. The superior acquirements of that nation doubtless might enable them to encounter those difficulties which have been mentioned, and either by their extensive conquests, or acknowledged commercial activity, to induce their language to be received as the general medium of intercourse. On the subject of this language, and its different dialects in these islands, some variety of opinion may be fairly allowed to prevail; and Sir W. Jones, Dr. Wilkins, Mr. Marsden, Mr. Raffles, and other authorities, may not be decided as to its source; but it is generally allowed that the language spoken by the Papuans, Samangs, and Negritos of the Philippines, and adjacent islands, is totally different from the Malayan; and as Mr. Marsden expresses himself, "presents a subject of research as curious as it is obscure."

This latter gentleman, in the ingenious introduction to his valuable grammar of the Malayan language, says, that the large islands of this archipelago have their own peculiar language spoken by the inhabitants of the interior, while the Malayan is generally used in the districts bordering on the coasts, at the mouths and on the banks of navigable rivers, and has thence acquired the appellation of the Lingua Franca of the east. The antiquity of this insular or original language, we are, he says, without the means of ascertaining; but he well supports its stability by the strong proof he adduces of Pigafetta's Vocabulary of the Tidore language, in 1521, differing in no respect from that of the present day. Mr. Marsden seems to conclude that the Malay population of this archipelago has its root in Sumatra, the inhabitants of which island claim immediate descent from some of the companions of Noah, landed there from the ark; and both Mr. Marsden, and Mr. Raffles, the present Governor of Java, assert, that the language spoken in Sumatra differs in no material respect from that spoken in the Malayan peninsula.

Upon any occasion where additional light could be thrown upon the subject of these islands, the translator has not scrupled to avail himself of the best authorities for that purpose. The *Voyage de Sonnerat aux Indes orientales et a la Chine,* edited and enlarged by Sonnini, has been of great service in this respect, as containing the most authentic information which was possible to be procured by a foreigner, aided by every facility which the influence of the court of France over that of Madrid could furnish, and entering upon the undertaking with the express intention of seconding the views of France on the colonial establishments of her European neighbours.

The translator hopes that, on the whole, the notes and extracts will not be found unimportant or useless.

On the subject of the map of the Philippines, accompanying this work, the translator trusts he will be excused expressing the gratification he feels in presenting it to the world as the only correct delineation of these islands in existence. A collection of the existing authorities he found answered no purpose, as being at variance not only with each other, but still more with the unpublished manuscript, and other authentic information he derived from the most competent private sources. To John Barrow, Esq. second Secretary, and Captain Hurd, Hydrographer to the Admiralty, he feels greatly indebted for the communications they favoured him with, and for amenity and politeness which accompanied them. To the first eastern scholar in this country, probably in Europe, Dr. Wilkins, Librarian to the East India Company, he owes more obligations than he can express. He takes this opportunity of expressing his gratitude for the kind assistance afforded by Captain Horsburgh, Hydrographer to the East India Company, who has had full opportunity, for the exercise of his practical and theoretical acquirements as a navigator in the eastern Archipelago, and who surveyed the western coasts of these islands, and in particular the northern extremity of the island of Luzon; to him he owes the correction of many errors, in respect to latitude and longitude, which disgrace the existing charts; and to him likewise the map is indebted, for a more perfect delineation of the coasts, and for the disappearance of certain dangerous rocks which he has ascertained to have no existence. From these sources, aided by the suggestions of commanders in the India service, in regard to the nautical part, and from John Guise, Esq. of Baker-street, whose residence of nine years in Manila afforded him ample means of information respecting the interior of Luzon, the map, it is presumed, may be deemed the most correct extant. To this latter gentleman he has to acknowledge further obligations on the score of the general information he has kindly furnished. To his friend, John Jackson, Esq. whose literary attainments do him so much honour, the translator is under particular obligations for the kind assistance afforded him in regard to the map. To Peter Guichenet, Esq. he feels particularly indebted, as well as to another friend, for the permission to extract from his excellent manuscript translation of *Sonnerat* as much as answered his purpose.

The merit of a translator is very limited. He is answerable for little beyond the actual transfusion of his author's meaning in appropriate language: whatever the present translator has attempted beyond this is contained in the notes, and is added with the hope of rendering the publication as valuable as possible, and as replete with information on the religious, moral, political, and commercial state of these dependencies on the Spanish crown as the existing sources are capable of furnishing. He lays it before the public with diffidence, but with the hope that it will add to the stock of general knowledge; equally useful to the moralist, the politician, and the merchant.

PHILIPPINE ISLANDS.

CHAPTER I.

Their Description—Productions and Commerce.

THE Philippine Islands were so named by Ruy Lopez de Villalobos, in compliment to Philip the Second, when Prince of Asturias. They originally were called the Western Isles, or the Archipelago of Saint Lazarus, the name which Magellan gave them when first discovered by him. These islands are numerous; their appearance on the map is that of a large blanket full of holes and rents. The principal of them is *Luzon*, so called, because at the doorway of each house stands a large wooden mortar, which, in the language of the country, is called *Losong*, and in which the Indians wash their rice. This island resembles the arm a little bent, and in the part which corresponds to the elbow is situated the city of Manila, on the shore of a fine bay, thirty leagues in circumference, and which receives some considerable rivers, among others the Pasig, which flowing from a large lake, situated to the east of Manila, at the distance of three leagues, washes its walls on the north side: its water is very soft and salubrious.

Before the Spaniards arrived this district was occupied by the nation Tagala, inhabiting many towns and mud villages, governed by petty chiefs. It is now divided into various provinces, under the government of their respective Alcaldes Mayores, who collect the royal tribute, and administer justice among the Indians. At three leagues distance from Manila, to the south-west, lies the port of Cavite, so called from the word *cauit*, a fish-hook, to which the tongue of land on which it stands bears a strong resemblance. Cavite is defended by an indifferent fort, the governor of which is nominated by the court of Madrid. It is likewise provided with a complete arsenal for the accommodation, as well of the Acapulco ships, and a few small vessels for the defence of the islands from the Moors, as for general use.

To the north from the nation Tagala, we found the nations Pampanga, Zambales, Pangasinan, Ylocos, and Cagayan. Each of these nations formed a distinct community, with a distinct language, or dialect of the same language, and was distributed in mud villages, having no king or supreme head to govern them; but in lieu of that, a number of petty chiefs, or rajahs, whose authority scarcely extended over fifty or an hundred families respectively: after the conquest, each of these nations was constituted into a province, governed by a Spanish Alcalde Mayor. To the east from the nation Tagala are the Camarines, whose district has been divided into two provinces, that of Camarines, and that of Albay, each under an Alcalde Mayor. The greater part of the island is mountainous; it is crossed from the north to the south by an immense chain, from which diverge those ramifications that spread through the whole island, in many cases even forming detached mountains, like insulated cones in the midst of extensive plains. The whole of this elevated part of the country occupying nearly all the interior, is either a desert, or inhabited by a set of wretched people who do not acknowledge the Spanish government. There are in this island several volcanos, as that of Mayon, which is between the provinces of Albay and Camarines. It has a sugar-loaf figure, and is of such altitude that it may be discovered at an immense distance at sea. The de Taal is of a similar form, and stands in the middle of a large lake, called de Bombon; it exhibits sufficient proof that the mountain in whose top the volcano was, while in its active state, has sunk, remaining, however, still pretty much elevated above the water. There are other volcanos, and many warm springs, indicating the fermentation in the bowels of this island, from which, no doubt, arise those earthquakes to which it is subject, and which, one day, may produce new eruptions. We know that these volcanos at times throw out ashes, stones, sand, water, and lava, inundating and destroying the habitations, and rendering the fields a desert.

To the south of Luzon lie the principal islands of Mindoro, Panay, Marinduque, Negros, Masbate, Zebu, Bohol, Leyte, Samar, besides some very small ones, the whole of which we denominate Bisayas, or Islas de Pintados, Painted Islands, their inhabitants having been accustomed to paint their bodies before our arrival in this quarter. All these islands acknowledge the Spanish government, and pay tribute to the king, which the corregidores, or Alcaldes Mayores of the provinces into which they are divided, collect. More to the south from these islands are Mindanao and Jolo. In Mindanao the provinces of Misamis and Caraga are subject to the Spaniards: the rest of the island has not submitted, and is engaged with Jolo and other islands in constant hostility against them; and although there have been occasional intervals of peace, they have been of short duration.

For these two centuries past these islanders have been plundering the coasts of our provinces, have taken an immense number of vessels, pillaged many villages, burnt many towns, destroyed many inhabitants, and made slaves of a very great number of the clergy, both Spaniards and Indians[1].

We have in Mindanao the garrison of Zamboanga, with a Spanish governor, to check these depredations; but as yet we have found little benefit from this establishment.

To the east of these islands, at the distance of three hundred leagues, are found las Marianas, las Carolinas, and the islands de Palaos, or Pelew. Of these, the Marianas alone are under the dominion of the Spaniards. Here there is a governor, with a detachment of troops, to overawe the Indians, and three Franciscan friars to instruct them in the Christian religion.

These islands have no other communication with the rest of the world than what is afforded by the Acapulco ship, which, in returning to Manila, touches there, with the portion of the revenue appropriated to the support of this presidency. By this opportunity they likewise receive wine for mass, grain, furniture, clothing, and a few other necessaries; this obscure corner producing only horned cattle, hogs, fowls, and a few vegetables, such as the bread-fruit and others, which serve the inhabitants instead of bread. These supplies are annually imported by the governor; and as there is no other store in the island than his, the price he fixes is at his own option. From this commerce he draws all his income; and under such oppression it is not to be wondered at that this colony is as poor as the first day it was discovered[2]. Rice, Indian corn, and wheat would grow abundantly in these islands, but every attempt to raise them in any quantity, has been rendered of no avail by the swarms of rats, which pour down from the mountains, and sweep all before them. From the combination of these political and natural causes, the situation of the inhabitants of these islands is so miserable, that some of our historians would persuade us, they entertain no wish to propagate the species, that their children may avoid their unhappy lot. On this account, it is added, the Indians diminish considerably in number; but this seems to be a mistake, as the diminution of the Indians, if it may be so called, may be rather attributed to the following cause.

The population of the Marianas, independent of the native Indians, consists of many from New Spain, some Philippine Indians, and some Chinese, who come in the suite of the governors. These men being married to women of the country, the children born of these marriages, are registered by the friars on a list of casts, distinguished from the Indian casts, from which it clearly appears that, in proportion as these mixed casts have increased, the Indian casts must have diminished, and, in all probability, in a short time this latter cast will be annihilated, as has already happened in some of the Spanish settlements. This being the case, we ought not to say the Indians diminish but change their cast. With all these casts united, our historians would wish us to believe, that there are, at present, fewer inhabitants in the Marianas than formerly; but that cannot be the case, since the Jesuits, in quitting these islands, left a greater population than they found in the year 1738; and the Franciscans report that that has increased progressively since. It is certain the population does increase, as is clearly shewn by the lists of the casts. Indeed the inhabitants of the Philippines have doubled every century; and I believe it is the case with all the population of America, although foreigners charge us, with occasioning the diminution of the Indian population, by our oppressive and bad management, quoting our own historians in support of the charge. It ought to be recollected, however, that by these, the number of inhabitants which the Spaniards found on their arrival, is considerably exaggerated, whenever they are desirous of giving additional splendor to the actions of the heroes they celebrate; and, on the contrary, when it is their object to detract, they draw a very opposite picture, and, attempting to diminish their numbers, assert that their diminution is the consequence of oppression. From the amount of the tributes, however, referred to by these historians, and levied at different times, the evident conclusion is, that the Spaniards did not find the tenth part of the inhabitants, which are now in existence.

The geographical description of the Philippines is, that they are in the torrid zone, between five and nineteen degrees of northern latitude; the sun twice passes its zenith, and produces those vapours which, descending in copious showers, and being again absorbed by the earth, form fountains, hot springs, and large lakes. This rainy or wet season lasts while we have the Sun to the north, that is, from about May till September, and at times till the beginning of December, from which latter period till May there is continual spring. The regular winds are the north, the east, and the south-west, and they each prevail beween three and four months at a time, the change of one wind for another, being attended with violent storms of thunder, lightning, and, at times, whirlwinds. Indeed these storms are complete hurricanes, which run all round the compass in less than twenty-four hours, tearing up trees by the roots, and laying waste the whole country. These are so frequent, that we may justly complain, considering our proximity to the line, of the want of sufficient solar influence, to render the climate of these islands more agreeable. It cannot be said that we have oppressive heat in the Philippines[3]; there reigns throughout the greater part of the year, a most beautiful spring, and if the atmosphere were less moist, it would be the most delicious climate in the world. To this moist atmosphere, and moderately warm temperature, is joined of course a great fertility. The trees are always covered with leaves, and the soil with vegetation. The harvests of rice are most abundant; the plants shoot up with great beauty immediately, but the luxuriance of the soil renders it necessary, continually to clear away the weeds, which harbour many insects of a destructive kind, and others so dangerous as to diminish greatly the comforts and enjoyments of a country, which, in point of fertility, returns one hundred fold of rice, the common food of the Indians.

Rice is the principal production of these islands, and it was cultivated to much greater extent before the Spaniards arrived here[4]. They have likewise some pulse, as mongos, patani, kidney-beans, and millet. The inhabitants breed up, under the same roof with themselves, pigs, fowls, ducks, goats, and even buffaloes. In the mountains there are many deer, and the woods and fields produce all sorts of pigeons, small birds, quails, a species of partridge, woodcocks, &c. Few are disposed to indulge themselves in this latter kind of sporting; they apply themselves ardently to hunting the deer, to which they are particularly partial. The sea abounds with very rich fish, such as the pargo, the eel, the sole, the pampano, the mojarra, the garropa, the shad, the tunny, the corvina, the tanguingui, and an infinite number of others, caught either with hooks or common nets, and likewise with a species of net very much used in these rivers, and even out at sea, so constructed that the fish may enter, but are unable to escape.

In this occupation the inhabitants of these islands take more delight than in any thing else, as it is a pursuit which at once indulges their indolent habits, and gratifies their partiality to fish in preference to animal food. Throughout the country are found many other productions, contributing to the support of life, and which, though not so relishing as those enumerated above, are probably better suited to their relaxed habits; and the pith of the palm, shoots of the sugar-cane, green withs, and other succulent productions, serve for food to those, who have no desire to labour for their subsistence. They cultivate the bread-fruit, beans, the cacauate, &c. and they pay particular attention to the palm tree, from which they procure both a spirit and an oil, together with a sweetmeat, which they call chancaca. There are few fruit-trees, and those are bad, with the exception of the plantain, of which there is a great variety, and all excellent and fine flavoured, and the orange, of which there are two kinds. The mango, a very rich fruit, it is imagined, the Spaniards imported from the coast of South America. We finish our enumeration with the cultivation of a species of the palm tree, which bears a very hard, little fruit of the form of a green nut.

This being cut, a highly scented kernel, or eye, is found enclosed, which is called *Itmo.* This is laid in lime, to make what they call *Buyo,* which being chewed, produces a red saliva, together with a disorder in the mouth, to which they are so habituated, that they are uneasy when without it. This custom prevails generally, and even many Spaniards adopt it with great avidity. There are in this country mines of iron and gold, but of little value, either from the indolence of the natives, or the insignificance of these objects to the Spaniards, affording too little profit in their commerce with Acapulco to deserve attention. Gold is likewise, by washing, separated from the sand, which the waters bring down from the mountains.

In Paracale they work the mines in the same manner as they do in New Spain, but the natives are so addicted to sloth, it is not possible to render them so productive as those of South America. In the mountains there is excellent timber for building ships or houses, and the canes are of an immense size, very long, and as thick as a man's thigh; of these latter the Indians construct their houses, covering them with the leaf of the palm. They raise cotton for clothing, which they dye various colours with logwood, indigo, and the achiote, a large tree, whose seed is used for that purpose. There is great abundance of wax and wild honey, amber, pearls, mother of pearl, marble, tar, brimstone, and many other objects of less value in a commercial point of view.

To these productions the Spaniards have added horses and horned cattle, which have multiplied so much that they are to be found in the mountains without an owner, and where those that want may supply their wants at pleasure. They likewise introduced sheep, geese, grapes, figs, wheat, pepper, coffee, cocoa, sugar, tobacco, and various species of plants, which thrive so well, and produce so much, that the Indian, with all his sloth, acknowledges the utility of cultivating them.

There are, in these islands, some natural curiosities deserving particular notice, such as the paxarillo, a species of small swallow, which forms its nest chiefly of the froth of the sea[6], and which is held in such estimation by the Chinese, as a principal dish at their table, that they purchase it at any price.

The *Balate* is a species of sea worm, which, likewise, is sold in China at a high price. The *Siguey*, is a small shining shell[7], which forms the current money of the Malays. The *Tabon*, is a bird, which lays eggs similar to those of the turkey, burying them very deep in the sand on the sea shore, and when hatched by the heat of the sun, it tears away the sand that covers them, and the young come out. The *Caiman*, is a species of crocodile; a large and uncouth animal, the more curious in this respect, that it is produced from an egg, of the same size as that of the duck. The *Chacon*, is a lizard, which takes up its abode in the houses, and repeatedly articulates clearly the word *toco*. The *Calo*, is a bird, which has a kind of hollow shell in his head, and crows, at certain hours of the day, the same as the cock. The *Taclobo*, is a large species of the oyster, the shell of which will hold a pitcher of water; indeed they are used as vessels for holy water in the churches. Our historians mention many curiosities even more rare than these, but I do not enumerate them, as they seem to have been ill informed on the subject, and I fear with good reason, having been too much under the influence of the marvellous, they have given credit to the Indians, who are always desirous of distinguishing themselves by the relation of something very uncommon.

With all these productions, the Indians formed a species of commerce, or barter, among each other, still considering gold as the representative of general value, or medium of exchange; they were likewise in the habit of trading with the Chinese, and with the Moors of Borneo, for flag-stones, copper, articles of furniture, &c. but in very small quantities, their wants being necessarily few, going almost naked, baking their rice in green canes, and eating it with the leaf of the plantain.

The Spaniards, soon after they came into possession of these islands, commenced an extended commerce with India and China, which brought to New Spain, a proportionable increase of profit; and in a little time, Manila became so rich a colony, that it created a jealousy among the merchants of Seville, and, in consequence of their petition, its commerce was restricted. From this period it began to decline, and to the great detriment of these islands, which cannot subsist by the exchange of their own productions alone, these being very limited in their nature, and incapable of much extension, surrounded as they are by other nations, more industrious, and who can work at a cheaper rate[8].

The luxuriant nature of the soil of these islands, has been much and justly extolled, but, proper allowance has not been made, for the sloth of the Indians, the hurricanes or tempests, which sweep every thing before them, the destructive insects, the rats, and many other things, which diminish greatly the fertility of these beautiful islands[9].

CHAPTER II.

Of the Inhabitants the Spaniards found in the Philippines—their Language, Customs, and Religion.

Our historians, affecting always the marvellous, divide into different classes, the inhabitants the Spaniards found, on their first arrival in the Philippines. They denominate them satyrs, men with tails, sea monsters, and whatever else of the fabulous, is calculated to raise wonder in the human mind. In reality, however, they found only two classes, that which we know by the appellation of Negroes, and that of the Indians. The Negroes are very small in stature, and more of a copper colour than those of Guinea, with soft hair and flat noses. They lived in the mountains, almost in a state of nature, merely covering the forepart of the body, with a piece of the bark of a tree; and they subsisted upon roots, and such deer, as in hunting, they could kill with the bow and arrow, at which they were very dexterous. They slept where night overtook them, and they possessed no idea of religion or civilized habits, rather, indeed, ranking with beasts than as human beings. The Spaniards, have at length succeeded, in domesticating many of them, and converting them to christianity, to which they give no opposition, so long as they get subsistence, but if they are obliged to labour, for the maintenance of their family, they return again to the mountains.

The Negroes, without doubt, were the primitive inhabitants of these islands, and they retired to the mountains, on the arrival of the Indians. These latter, settling on the sea shore, continual hostility prevailed between them, but the Indians were never able, to establish themselves sufficiently, to be permitted, even to cut wood in the mountains, without paying a tribute for it. At present, the influence of the Negroes is very limited, but their antipathy to their first invaders, continues unabated; for, if a Negro is killed, or dies suddenly, it is customary for another, to bind himself to his countrymen by an oath, that he will disappear from among them, and that he will not return, until he has avenged the death of his friend, by killing three or four Indians, to accomplish which, he watches their villages, and the passes in the mountains, and if any unfortunately stray from their companions, he murders them.

The origin of these Negroes, some believe to be, from Angola[10], though they are not so black as their ancestors, which it is pretended, proceeds from the temperature of these islands being milder, and less scorching than that of Africa. This possibly may be so, for it is well known, that by changing, from a sultry to a temperate climate, the blackness of the Negro may be diminished, in the course of a long series of generations; yet, the flat nose, and using a dialect of the same language, which the Indians of these isles speak, appears to prove satisfactorily enough, that the origin of one and the other, is nearly the same. The reason assigned, for their not being more numerous, is, the influence of the rain, wind, sun, and all those inclemencies natural to the climate, to which they are exposed; the errors of the government, having reduced them to the condition, almost, of wild beasts, in which we now see them[11]. The Indians whom the Spaniards found here, were of regular stature, and of an olive complexion, with flat noses, large eyes, and long hair. They all possessed some description of government better or worse, and each nation was distinguished by a different name; but, the similarity of their dress and manners, proves that the origin of all of them is the same.

They had chiefs, who held their situations, either on account of personal valour, or by succession to their fathers, where they had abilities to retain it. Their dominion extended over one or two villages, or more, according to the means they possessed, of extending protection. They were continually at war with the neighbouring villages, and continually making each other slaves. Out of these wars, arose three classes of people; the chiefs or masters of the villages, the slaves, and those whom the chiefs had enfranchised, with their descendants, and who, to this day, are called Timavas, properly signifying children of liberty. In some places, were found Indians whiter than others, descended, without doubt, from Chinese or Japanese, who had been shipwrecked on these coasts, and whom the Indians, naturally hospitable, received, and allowed to intermarry with them; and it is generally believed that the Ygorrotes of Ylocos, whose eyes resemble the Chinese, must have originated from the companions of Limahon, who fled to those mountains, when Juan de Salcedo compelled him to his disgraceful retreat, from the province of Pangasinan.

It is not, however, after all, easy to ascertain the origin of these people, but their idiom throws some degree of light on the subject. Although the languages these Indians speak, are many and different, they have so much intercourse one with another, that it may clearly be discovered, they are dialects of the same language, as the Spanish, French, and Italian, are derivatives from the Latin. The prepositions and pronouns, are nearly the same in all of them; the numeral characters, differ very little, and they have many words in common, and of one and the same structure.

No doubt can be entertained, that the radical language, from which all those dialects spring, prevails from Madagascar to the Philippines, with local shades of difference. It is spoken too in New Guinea, and in all the islands to the southward, in the Marianas, in the islands of San Duisk, in those of Otaheite, and in almost all the islands in the South Sea. In one collection of voyages, there are given various vocabularies, with such corresponding terminations, as the respective travellers, were able to distinguish among these islands. It is remarkable, that in these almost all the pronouns, are the same with those of the nation Tagala; the numerals, are common to all the dialects, used in these islands, and most of the words are the same, and with the same signification, as in the language Tagala. But, I am the more inclined to believe the identity of the dialects, from a conversation which I had with Don Juan Hovel, an Englishman, who spoke that of San Duisk, and who had a slave, a native of one of those islands. The structure, appeared to be the same, as that of the languages spoken in the Philippines; and on the whole, I feel confident in the opinion, that they are all dialects of the same language, so widely diffused over so large a portion of the earth. It is ascertained, that this language, is in common use for many thousand leagues, extending from Madagascar to the isles ofSan Duisk, Otaheite, and the isle of Pasquas, which latter, is not more than six hundred leagues distant, from the coast of South America. Yet, the Indians of the Philippines, do not understand the people of these last mentioned islands, when they have occasional intercourse with them; nor, even in these islands, do the inhabitants of one province, understand those of another. So neither does the Spaniard understand the Frenchman, nor the Frenchman the Italian.

In the same collection of voyages, already referred to, we find a vocabulary of only five terminations, which the Spaniards have distinguished on the coast of Patagonia, and which they have been able to assimilate to the language of these islands, and one of those is the word *balay*, which in that country signifies a house; and by this same word they designate a house among the Pampangos, and the inhabitants of the Bisayas in general. This may be more matter of accident than of proof, that the languages of one and the other is the same; but on observing, besides this, that the proper names of places about the middle of the continent of South America are very similar to those of the Philippines, I endeavoured to procure a vocabulary of this country, and did not fail to examine, with great diligence and attention, the few words of the language of Chili which Ercilla mentions in his Araucana, and which I found perfectly conformable to the language Tagala. The name Chili is a derivation from this language: the Cormorant is called Cachile, and this is a name which the Malays give to the sons of their kings. Chilian, which is a town of Chili, is a compound from the language of Tagala, in which language the termination *an* gives the signification *town*. Thus from Cachile we draw Cachilian, meaning a town, where there are cormorants. Mapocho, which is the situation where the city of Santiago stands, is another word of Tagalic composition, signifying a town, and pocquiot being a kind of herb, we form the name Mapocquiot, a town in which there is abundance of this herb.

In Chili they frequently double the syllables in forming a word, as ytayta, biobio, lemolemo, colocolo, &c. and this occurs in the Tagala language; for instance, we say ataata, bilobilo, lebomlebom, colocolo. A great many other words are either actually of Tagalic derivation, or assimilate closely to that language. In examining the structure of these two languages we are compelled to conclude that they flow from one and the same source, and I dare affirm that the Indians of the Philippines are descended from the aborigines of Chili and Peru, and that the language of these islands derives immediately from the parent source, those of the neighbouring islands being dialects of this. Many will urge the absurdity of this supposition, on the plea that the more immediate vicinity of the Philippines to Malacca must have occasioned them to be colonized by the Malays, as our historians generally assert. I do not deny that these islands could easily have been peopled by the Malays, but how could they colonize the Isles de Palaos and Marianas, which are distant more than three hundred leagues? and it is still more improbable that they colonized the islands of San Duisk and Otaheite, which are distant two thousand leagues from the Philippines. All these people, however, have the same language, the same manners and customs, and consequently the same origin as our Indians. There is, in my opinion, this other reason for supposing these latter islands could not be peopled from the westward, viz. that in all the torrid zone the east wind generally prevails, which being in direct opposition to the course from Malacca and the adjacent islands, it is fair to conclude that the inhabitants of all the islands of the South Sea came from the east, sailing before the wind; for we have seen it often happen, that the Indians from the Palaos have arrived at the Philippines, precisely under those circumstances. On the contrary, we have no instance on record, of any of the Philippine Indians having been, even by accident, carried by the winds to the islands to the eastward. Indeed we know the reverse of this to be true, since at times the most experienced pilots, in attempting this navigation, have been compelled to return, without falling in with the islands they went in search of, from the necessity there is in the voyage of being provided with proper nautical instruments,

Here, therefore, we appear to have found the most probable solution of our difficulties, that is, that the first settlers came out of the east, we may presume from the coast of South America, and proceeding gradually to the westward through the Pacific Ocean, studded as we find it with islands, and clusters of islands, at no very great distance from each other, and of course of easy access before the wind, it follows that to whatever point, in an eastern direction, we can trace the Tagalic language, we may conclude that at that point emigration must have commenced. Some however dissent from this, on the ground, that the mode of writing in use among the Malays, is similar to that practised by the inhabitants of the Philippines. This consists in forming the lines from the right to the left, like the Arabians, Persians, &c. and not like the Chinese, Tartars, and Japanese, from top to bottom. Their characters are totally different from ours; they have only three vowels, *a*, *e*, *u*, and by placing a point either above or below the consonant, or leaving it without one, the corresponding vowel is readily known, and equal facility given as if the vowels were specifically inserted. Although they can write, they have no written laws; decisions are made on traditionary law generally, but too often by the right of the strongest. The Rajah, or chief, with the assistance of some of the elders, decides in all civil cases; but in criminal cases, the kinsmen are accustomed to compound with the aggressor, for a sum in gold, unless in cases of murder, when the only atonement admitted, is retaliation; and if the murderer is of a different tribe or village, all the community of which the deceased was a member, make a common cause, against the tribe or community of the murderer, and numbers are generally made slaves on both sides. When it is suspected that one man has robbed another, he is obliged to

D 2

draw a stone, from the bottom of a cauldron full of boiling water, and if he does not accomplish this, which is the vulgar test, he is fined in a certain quantity of gold, the greater part of which goes to the Rajah or chief. Adultery is likewise punished with a pecuniary fine[12], as is the crime of disrespect to the elders, but for fraud, and cheating in their dealings, there is no punishment, and usury is very general among them. Their matrimonial customs are peculiar; they are allowed to marry only one woman, and although the principal people have several concubines, yet they commonly are slaves. They are accustomed to marry a relation (not a sister), with whom if they find themselves unable to live, or if they become tired of her, they return her to her parents, without their being required to assign a cause for the divorce. The dowry given on the day of marriage is merely restored: this dowry is of two kinds, and which the bridegroom always pays.

The one is called *bigay suso*, and is paid to the mother, as a compensation for the milk, with which she nourished her daughter. The other is called *bigay caya*, or green dowry, which is set apart for the maintenance of the newly married couple, although very often, by the expences of the wedding and apparel, there remains little or nothing for this desirable end. Besides these dowries paid by the bridegroom, he is obliged, for some years, to serve the parents of the bride [13], and assist them on certain days, particularly at the sowing of the rice, and getting in the harvest. It is incumbent likewise, on all the relations of the bridegroom, to behave with courtesy and respect to the bride, and her parents and family, during these years of service, and if they are guilty of any lapse in this respect, the marriage is declared to be annulled, which is always very agreeable to the parents of the woman, as a new suitor presents himself, and they reap the benefit of a new service. The bridegroom, to console himself for his sufferings, as soon as the term closes, and his service is at an end, treats his wife as a slave; she is obliged to work for the maintenance of the family, whilst the husband is quite idle, and thinks herself happy, if, after having done this, she is not beaten. The interest which the parents of the girl, thus have in her disposal, is highly pernicious to morals; and we have not succeeded to this hour, in the abolition of it, either by the influence of royal edicts, or the regulations of the bishops, by both of which, it is discouraged and prohibited. The ceremony of marriage is performed, by sacrificing a hog, which a priestess slays with a thousand grimaces; after which, she bestows many benedictions on the parties, and an old woman presenting them with some food, the ceremony is closed by many obscenities. Dancing, according to their fashion, succeeds, and drinking the rest of the day ends the feast, which is always proportionate to the circumstances of the newly married pair. The principal contributions to this feast, arise from presents made to the bride and bridegroom by their friends, of which particular notice is taken, in order that similar presents, may be returned to the parties on a like occasion.

In their religious ceremonies, they use neither idols nor temples; their sacrifices are offered in arbours, which they raise for that purpose. They have priestesses, whom they call *babailanas* or *catalonas*, to whose function it belongs, to perform the sacrifices. The priestess, taking a lance in her hand, with extravagant and ridiculous gestures, works herself up to apparent frenzy, accompanied by foaming at the mouth, when uttering something, which is received as prophecy, she pierces the hog with the lance, and immediately distributes the carcase among those present: the ceremony, as usual, is closed by dancing and drinking.

These sacrifices are offered to the infernal deities, as well as to the souls of their ancestors, who they are taught to believe inhabit very large trees, rocks of uncommon appearance, or any natural object which, in point of magnitude or form, varies from the usual course. They are so fully persuaded of this, that they never pass any object of this description, without first asking the permission of its visionary inhabitant, and to this hour the custom prevails. When any person was dangerously ill, his friends offered up to their deities rice, wine, and flesh, which was then given to the sick person, and which they were of opinion would effect his cure, a custom even yet followed by some people. They have many other superstitions, as that of the *patianac*, a spirit or ideal being, whose employment or amusement consists in preventing, by certain means peculiar to itself, the delivery of a woman in labour. To counteract the malignity of this spirit, the husband, fastening the door, reduces himself to a state of complete nudity, lights a fire, and arming himself with his sword, continues to flourish it furiously, until the woman is delivered. The *tigbalang* is another object of which they stand in great awe. It is described as a phantom, which assumes a variety of uncouth and monstrous shapes, and interposes its authority, to prevent their performing the duties, prescribed by our religion.

These and other superstitions, formerly had extensive influence, and are still resorted to by impostors, who find their account in persuading those, who are silly enough to listen to them, that they are able to cure them of dangerous illness, or to recover any thing they may have lost, by having recourse to such absurdities; and so much do the love of life, and our own individual interests prevail, that although they believe these customs sinful, and although they do not entirely give credit to their efficacy, yet they put them in practice, because, they say, chance may be in their favour: this is a proof that as yet they are very superficial christians[14]. Indeed, all their religious impressions, seem rather the result of a slavish dread, than the effect of rational piety.

They practise no external adoration, and have no other form of address to their gods, than what has been mentioned. They do not believe, that the good will be rewarded, or the wicked punished, but they acknowledge the immortality of the souls of the deceased, and that they are capable of doing them mischief. They persuade themselves, that these retain all the natural wants incident to the mortal state, and accordingly, place on their tombs, clothes, arms, and food, and on the fourth day, when the funeral ceremony is performed, a vacant seat is left at the table for the deceased, whom they believe to be actually present, though not obvious to sight. To prove this, sand is strewed on the floor, on which the prints of the feet of the deceased are often found. This may be presumed, to be the pious trick of some of the friends, but it answers the purpose, of inducing a belief in the actual presence of the party; and in order to deprecate the injury he may do, offerings of eatables are made to him, and which ceremony, is perfectly conformable, to the cowardly and timorous nature of the Indians.

CHAPTER III.

ANNO DOM. 1519 to 1564.

Comprising the Discovery of the Philippines.

After the conquest of the Americas, and discovery of the South Sea, Hernando de Magellan, a Portuguese, affirmed there must be a communication with that sea by the antarctic pole, and proposed to his sovereign, to make the discovery by the route of the Moluccas. The king, Don Manuel of Portugal, either not believing there was such a passage, or prejudiced against Magellan, received his proposal with contempt. This disgusted him, and he came into Spain, where, at Saragossa, he was presented to Charles V., to whom he promised the complete discovery of the

Moluccas, and the adjacent islands, within the Spanish line of demarcation, by a distinct route from that used by the Portuguese, pursuing his object by the expected antarctic passage to the South Sea. By the brief of Pope Alexander VI., expedited at Rome the 4th of May 1493, Magellan secured a patent, attaching such discoveries to the crown of Castile. This brief enjoined, that the globe should be equally divided, by a line drawn from the north, by the isles of the Azores, towards the south, embracing the conquests, which formed the western boundaries of the Atlantic; the portion to the west, to belong to the crown of Spain, and leaving to the crown of Portugal, the hemisphere to the eastward of this line. Having discovered the Brazils, however, and the king of Portugal being desirous of preserving it, he requested his Holiness, that the line might be drawn, four hundred and sixty leagues more to the westward of the Azores, in order, that no other power, might interfere with that valuable acquisition. The line was so drawn on the map, and the Moluccas, were accordingly, placed out of the line of territory, thus appropriated to the Portuguese, and within that of Spain[15]: they were not able, however, at that time, to adjust the other point as to the route; but the Cape of Good Hope, interposing in their voyages to India, it was not doubted, that America might be like this hemisphere, and finish also in a cape, and passage to the South Sea. The desire of the Spaniards to take possession of the Spice Islands, or, as they were called, the Moluccas, instigated them to ascertain the truth of this conjecture; and a squadron of five ships, was fitted out for that purpose, viz. La Trinidad, in which Magellan himself embarked; San Antonio, La Concepcion, Santiago, and La Victoria;

the whole manned with two hundred and thirty-four men, and paid and victualled for two years.

Magellan sailed from Seville with this armament on the 10th of August 1519, and on the 13th of December he arrived at the Brazils, and coasting the land in quest of the expected passage to the South Sea, on Easter day, he entered the Bay of Saint Julian, in fifty degrees of south latitude, where he intended remaining, finding the winter had commenced in those regions. Here his people mutinied, upon an idea that their provisions were exhausted, and that it was impossible to discover the pass they were in search of. Magellan quelled this mutiny; but immediately after understood, that another had broken out in the ship San Antonio, and that the crew had murdered the commander, and confined his cousin Alvaro de Mesquita, who was made captain on the arrest of Juan de Cartagena. The leader on this occasion was Gaspar de Quezada, whom he ordered to be hanged; and setting on shore a Franciscan friar and Juan de Cartagena, on account of their turbulent disposition, he sailed in prosecution of his voyage, by the much desired pass to the South Sea. On the 1st of November 1520, he discovered the straits which bear his name; and having occupied twenty days in passing through them, he found himself in the South Sea with three ships, the Santiago having been wrecked, and having separated from the San Antonio, which his cousin commanded, and which, by the route of the coast of Guinea, returned to Spain. Magellan, with fair winds and pleasant weather, ploughed that sea, which never before had been navigated. Uninterrupted in the pursuit of his object, he discovered, on the Sunday of Saint Lazarus, a great number of islands, which he named the Archipelago of Saint Lazarus; and on Easter Day, he arrived at the island of Mindanao, where he ordered the first mass which was said in the Philippines. This took place in the town of Batuan, in the province of Caraga, where he set up the cross, and took possession of these islands, in the name of the King of Spain.

From Batuan, Magellan proceeded to Zebu, and, in passing the island of Dimasaua, he formed an alliance with its chief, who accompanied him to Zebu. The inhabitants of Zebu, received him with such kindness, that their king, Hamabar, his whole family, with the chief of Dimasaua, and many of the people of the island, were baptized. The King of Mactan alone, a very small island in front of the town of Zebu, resisted the Spaniards, and was sufficiently confident in his strength, to challenge Magellan, who was weak enough to accept the challenge. He selected for the enterprize fifty Spaniards, who attacked the Indians in morasses, the water up to their breasts, and approached so near them, that Magellan was wounded with an arrow, and died on the field with six other Spaniards, the rest saving themselves by flight.

The friar Calancha, an Augustine, remarks in his history of Peru, that all those engaged in the discovery of the South Sea, came to no very enviable end: for, that a seaman of the name of Lopez, who was the first that beheld it from the mast-head, renounced his faith, and turned Moor. Basco Nunez de Balbua, who took possession of those regions, lost his head; and Magellan himself, finished his days in the abovementioned manner. I can add, that almost all those, who have been concerned in the discovery of the Philippines, have suffered so much, that the history of these islands, forms a tissue of tragedies.

On the death of Magellan, the Spaniards chose Juan Serrano as Commander of the expedition; and, alarmed at their defeat at Mactan, they remained on board their ships, apprehensive of the treachery of the other Indians. In fact, the people of Zebu, began to think lightly of the strangers, whom they had hitherto considered as invincible, and proceeded to plan their destruction. Abundantly deceitful by nature, they concealed their designs, and succeeded in persuading our General to be present, with twenty-four Spaniards, at a feast, which the chief of Zebu had prepared for him. In the middle of the feast, a great number of armed Indians, whom Hamabar had concealed, rushed in, and murdered them all, Serrano alone excepted, who escaped to the sea side, and implored the assistance of his companions; but they, fearful of some new treason, were witnesses of his massacre, which the Indians effected in view of the squadron, without their attempting to relieve him, or revenge the injury. Juan Carvallo now became General of the armament, and he resolved to go from thence, in search of the Moluccas:

E 2

he burned the ship Concepcion, as he had not men sufficient to man her, and sailed from Zebu with the Trinidad and the Victoria. On the 8th of November he arrived at Tidore, one of the Moluccas, and was well received by its chief, who granted him a factory for the purpose of collecting cloves, &c.; and on the 21st of December, he loaded the two ships with spices, preparing for the return to Spain. Gonzalo Gomez de Espimosa commanded the Trinidad, and it was his intention to proceed to Panama, but he was captured by the Portuguese. Sebastian del Cano, went in the Victoria, by the way of the Cape of Good Hope, and, after losing many of his crew on the voyage, arrived at San Lucar de Barrameda, with only eighteen people, on the 7th of September 1522, three years from the time of their departure from Seville. He was thus the first, who had sailed round the world; and on this account, among other honours, the Emperor gave him for his arms, a terrestrial globe, with this motto, *Hic primus geometros.*

The account which Sebastian del Cano gave of the expedition, induced the Emperor, to send other armaments to the Moluccas. The first was that of Esteban Gomez, who proposed, by the way of Newfoundland, to discover a shorter passage to the South Sea. A squadron was accordingly despatched in the year 1524; but in a little time, news was received of its dispersion by bad weather. In the year following, Don Fray Garcia Jofre de Loaysa, was despatched from Corunna with seven ships, well appointed with good officers, and four hundred and fifty picked men; among these was Andres de Urdaneta, who afterwards became a friar of the order of San Augustine, and directed the expedition of Legaspi to these islands. They passed the Straits of Magellan, with the loss of one ship, and entering the South

Sea, they encountered so severe a storm, that the whole squadron was separated. Loaysa pursued his course; and in a short time afterwards died. By order of the Emperor, Sebastian del Cano was to succeed to the command, but he surviving only a few days, it devolved on Martin Yañez, a Biscayan. They arrived at Tidore on the 31st of December 1526, as did, in a short time, the remainder of the squadron, with few men, and those unserviceable. Here they found, that the Portuguese had declared war against the chief of Tidore, for having entertained the squadron of Magellan, and it was deemed on our part proper, to undertake the defence of those benefactors of the Spaniards. They had several encounters with the Portuguese, but of no moment, and few were killed on these occasions; but the number of sick increased considerably, from the length and hardships of the voyage; and from the humid nature of the climate, the whole were threatened with rapid dissolution; being therefore already reduced to one hundred and twenty, they constructed a fort, and surrounding it with a palisade, placed themselves under the command of Hernando de la Torre, who was chosen General after the death of Martin Yañez.

In this situation, were the remains of the armament under Loaysa found, when the Viceroy of Mexico, by orders from court, despatched to Molucca three ships, under the command of Alvaro de Saavedra, who arrived at these islands, by the route of the Ladrones, now called Marianas, of which he took possession, in the name of his Majesty the King of Spain, in the year 1528. Saavedra pursued his voyage to Tidore, where he found the hundred and twenty Spaniards, shut up in their fortress. They considered him, as an angel sent to their relief, in the extremity of misery: but this joy was of short duration, new quarrels springing up with the Portuguese, who had succeeded in destroying, nearly all the Spanish ships. They at last, however, commenced their voyage to New Spain. Twice they made the attempt, twice they were driven back; and they suffered so much, that the General, with many of the crews, fell a sacrifice; the few that remained, being compelled to submit to the Portuguese. This was a most lamentable conclusion of the expedition; but all our squadrons, having represented the Moluccas as extremely valuable, on account of their spices, war was on the point of being declared, between the two kingdoms, about the possession of them. The Spaniards alleged, that it could not be denied, these islands were in the line of demarcation of Spain; and the Portuguese, were unwilling to quit the spice trade, of which they were in possession, and which so much enriched the mother country. These differences were adjusted about the year 1529, the Emperor, renouncing his right to the Moluccas, for three hundred and fifty thousand ducats, by way of loan, advanced by the King of Portugal.

Thus abandoning the Moluccas, the Emperor turned all his thoughts to the conquest of the Western Isles, or Philippines. He despatched instructions to the Viceroy of Mexico, to send a squadron for that purpose, with directions not to stop at the Moluccas, in order to avoid creating jealousy among the Portuguese. In obedience to these orders from court, the Viceroy immediately fitted out five ships in the Puerto de Natividad, and nominated as Commander of the expedition, Ruy Lopez de Villalobos, directing him, to take with him four Augustine friars, for the conversion of the conquered inhabitants. The squadron sailed on the day of All Saints, in the year 1542, and arrived safe off the Philippines; but they were driven so much to leeward, by the south-west monsoon, prevalent at that time, that they were compelled to anchor at the island of Sarragan, which lies on the opposite coast of Mindanao, and at forty leagues distance. In this miserable island, they suffered so much from hunger, that Villalobos sent some of the smaller vessels, in search of provisions, to the other islands: but, their return being delayed beyond his expectation, he resolved to sail for the Moluccas, though it was in direct opposition to his orders, without having effected any other object, than administering baptism to one child. The Portuguese received him very ungraciously, and compelled him, immediately to make the best of his way to Spain. In passing Amboyna, he died of a deep melancholy, arising out of the disasters of the expedition, and the idea of having disobeyed the orders of his sovereign, which were, on no account to visit the Moluccas. By the death of the General, the whole armament was deranged; indeed it was, eventually, almost all annihilated; and the few Spaniards who remained, found means to embark in different Portuguese ships. The Augustine friars went to Goa, from whence they found a passage to Europe, and arrived at Lisbon in August 1549, seven years after they had departed from the Puerto de Natividad.

As his Catholic Majesty, was fully determined on the conquest of the Philippines, it is necessary to notice the title, by which he laid claim to them. Our writers have brought forward a number of arguments, to prove the right, which the Kings of Spain have to the Americas, and the islands they have conquered; but I find them very superficial, and only one incontestable document, by which our sovereigns hold these dominions, that is, the concession of the Roman Pontifs. It is now the received opinion of churchmen, that the Popes have not the power to make such grants, but at the period in question, the contrary opinion prevailed, and was generally acknowledged in the schools. Supported by this idea, then so universal, the Papal See, granted to the respective Kings, not only what they conquered, but, as we have seen, assumed the right, of even partitioning the globe.

CHAPTER IV.

ANNO DOM. 1564 to 1565.

Of the Conquest of Zebu, and Discovery of the Route to New Spain.

THE glory of conquering the Philippines, was reserved for his Catholic Majesty Philip II., by means of, the valour of Miguel Lopez de Legaspi, the prudence of the Augustine friars, and the skill of one of those friars, Andres de Urdaneta, who had been a captain in the armament of Loaysa, but subsequently took the habit of San Augustine in Mexico, in the year 1552. His Majesty issued an edict, encouraging and recommending an expedition, to be sent by the Viceroy of Mexico, to the western isles. Friar Urdaneta acquiesced in the will of his sovereign, and the Viceroy chose five other religious of the same order, viz. Andres de Aguirre, Martin de Rada, Lorenzo Ximenes (who died in the Puerto de Natividad), Diego Herrera, and Pedro Gamboa, with the view to a spiritual, as well as temporal conquest. This squadron was composed of two ships, one small galleon, and a patache (a vessel so called). The command was given to Miguel Lopez de Legaspi, a noble Biscayan, from whose valour and prudence, the Viceroy expected greater results, than had been obtained from the other expeditions. The fleet sailed from Puerto de Natividad on the 21st November, 1564, with sealed orders; and when about a hundred leagues from the coast, the seals being broken, they found directions to proceed to these islands. Urdaneta had formed his plan, on the idea conceived by the Viceroy of first making New Guinea, but, obliged to conform to the royal instructions, he shaped his course nearly due west, in order to arrive at the ninth degree of latitude, and from thence to run direct west, to demand the submission of those islands, which lie between the ninth and tenth degree, passing by the islands of Arrecifes and Matalotes, together with those of La Nublada and Rocapartida, the two latter being too far out of the track. On the 31st of December, the patache separated, as if by accident, and never rejoined the squadron; Don Alonzo de Arellano was her commander, and Lopez Martin, a Mulatto, the pilot; and there was reason to believe that the separation was intentional, as it afterwards proved, that they went to Mindanao, where, taking in a cargo of gold and spices, they proceeded to New Spain. The squadron pursued its course, and on the 9th of January, 1565, discovered an island, which Legaspi called Barbudos, because the inhabitants wore longer beards than the other Indians. On the 22d they discovered the islands Ladrones, where they remained some days, taking in water and purchasing fresh provisions, which they procured from the Indians, in exchange for European commodities, especially iron, an article in great esteem with them. These Indians pilfered whatever they could lay their hands on, and assaulted our people while procuring water; yet, many Spaniards were desirous of remaining among them, and petitioned the General to found a colony there, and despatch a ship to Acapulco for that purpose; but having no orders to that effect, he prosecuted his route on the 3d of February, and on the 13th discovered the Philippines. At Tandaya, and Abuyo, he attempted to make an amicable arrangement with the inhabitants, for provisions, making presents to them, and promising, that he would pay liberally for every thing; but he could only procure one fowl and one egg. The stock of provisions, was now, however, becoming so short, that he deemed it necessary, to run in more among the islands, in search of a supply. They arrived at Bohol, and found the Indians had retired to the mountains. They had behaved so kindly, in selling provisions to those, whom Ruy Lopez de Villalobos had sent for that purpose, that Legaspi was astonished at their reserve, and could not conceive the cause of this change, until the pilot of a Bornean vessel discovered it. This vessel was taken by Colonel Matheo del Sauz, in the following manner. The General, had sent him to reconnoitre the vessel, and the Borneans, little acquainted with Europeans and their customs, and believing they came to make prisoners of them, received them in a hostile manner with their cannon[16], killing one soldier, and wounding twenty. The Colonel returned their fire, and killed their captain; when part of the crew escaped, in a small boat, which they carry in the prow of their junk (the name they give their vessels), and the pilot, with six men, delivered themselves up, without further resistance. All this having taken place, without the knowledge or participation of the General, he was extremely solicitous, to do away the ill impression, which the transaction might make, and ordered them to restore the junk, with all the effects which they had taken; and which conduct so satisfied the Borneans, that they immediately declared publicly, they should interest themselves particularly, in favour of the squadron. They informed Legaspi, among other matters, that about two years since, some Portuguese of the Moluccas, had landed on their island, had been guilty of great extortion, and had done considerable injury to the inhabitants; and as they could not distinguish between the two nations, they had imagined that the people of his squadron were Portuguese.

Legaspi was aware, that it was necessary, above all things, to undeceive the Indians in this respect; he, therefore, earnestly requested the pilot of the Bornean vessel, to go on shore, and effect a reconciliation with the natives of Bohol, bringing on board the Rajah of the island, if possible. The Moor, in gratitude to the Spaniards, exerted himself, and returned on board with the Rajah, Sicatuna, who was persuaded to enter into an amicable understanding with them, to be consecrated and confirmed, in the manner usual with these islanders, which is thus; the parties entering into a treaty of friendship being bled at the arm, and the blood mixed with a little water, or spirit, they reciprocally drink each other's blood, so diluted, in token of amity. Legaspi, with this view, sent a soldier of the name of Santiago on shore, to go through the ceremony with Sicatuna; but the latter, thinking it below his dignity, to allow his blood to be drawn, with any but that of the General, ordered his son to take his place, promising, that the day following, he would proceed on board, and be bled

F 2

island, against whose natives, they seldom have been obliged to use fire-arms.

On Easter day, the 22d of April, Legaspi accordingly sailed from Bohol, and on Friday the 27th, he arrived at Zebu, when he immediately despatched an interpreter named Pacheco, to propose amity with the natives, and that the Rajah might be sent to conclude the terms. Tupas, who was then King of Zebu, immediately sent some of the chief men, requesting Legaspi would not fire his artillery, which would alarm the town : and he promised to see the General, although he had no such intention, merely wishing to gain sufficient time, for the inhabitants to retire into the mountains, with all their moveables. It appearing the following day, that Tupas did not comply with his promise, three notifications were, in the space of two hours, sent to him by a notary, accompanied by Friar Urdaneta, who had the title of Protector of the Indians; but he paid no attention to this, and placed troops on the shore, and in canoes, to resist the landing of the Spaniards. Legaspi then determined on the assault, and ordered his men to fire on the canoes and Indians, who were posted to oppose them; but they retreated with such rapidity, that when the Spaniards leaped on shore, no enemy was to be seen. They followed them to the town, and found it in flames, the moveables having been taken away, and carried to the mountains, and little of any value remaining. The soldiers plundered those houses, which as yet, were not on fire, and among some things of little importance, they found a jewel, consisting of the image of a child, which they understood, was an object of adoration with the Indians, and which is at this day, in the church of San Augustine de Santo Niño of Zebu. The Indians, it appeared, had been in possession of this image, from time immemorial; and they were accustomed, when they wanted rain, to make a solemn feast, and public supplication to it, and, carrying it to the sea side, they immersed it in the water until it rained; honours or stripes, followed the concession or refusal, of what they had petitioned for, and it was believed among them, that this Santo Nino was the cause of the disgrace of Magellan. At first, the Spaniards found very few eatables in Zebu, but continuing their search, they stumbled upon thirty fanegas of rice, and some millet. In returning from the town, they encountered three hundred armed Indians; but upon our musquets being fired, they fled immediately. The General established his camp on the sea shore, and took out the Royal treasure which came in the Capitana, in order to be enabled to examine her bottom, and put her in a proper state, for her return to New Spain. The Spaniards found themselves perfectly secure in this encampment, in the day-time, because the Indians dared not attempt to molest them, through fear of their fire-arms; but at night, they occasioned them continual alarms, and on several occasions, set fire to their camp, doing however, little damage to the soldiers, who were defended by the palisades. The General however, in consequence of this, ordered the whole to be destroyed, and built a fort, which at once checked all further attempts. As yet, Legaspi kept on the defensive, expecting that Tupas would soon arrive, with whom he was desirous of being in amity, with a view to the conquest of the island by fair means. After repeated messages he at last appeared, accompanied by another chief, called Tamayan. Legaspi received them with cordiality, treated them handsomely, and, in the name of his sovereign, forgave the treachery, they had been guilty of towards Magellan. They made many excuses for their conduct, and promised that in three days they would return, with all the principal people, and establish a friendly intercourse with the Spaniards. These people will readily promise, whatever is demanded of them, but without any intention of performing their promise. Tupas, though King of the island, did not appear better entitled to respect, than any of the rest, and thought nothing of breaking his word, always, however, making some excuse on the succeeding visit.

Notwithstanding the peaceable demeanor of the Indians, the General ordered, that no one should be permitted to quit the camp, as he apprehended an ambuscade, which might have a fatal issue. This, in fact, happened to Pedro de Arana, one of Legaspi's aides-de-camp, who, disregarding this order, passed the lines alone with his gun, and before he was able to save himself, he was run through with a lance, and his head cut off, and carried on board a parao, which was lying at a little distance. The General felt the loss of Pedro de Arana much, and gave orders to the

Colonel, to chastise the insolence of the Indians, and reduce them. Whilst the Colonel was employed in this expedition, the General, who had been accustomed to sleep on board ship, determined to pass his nights on shore in future, through some distrust he entertained, of the officers of the navy, and ordered, that his aides-de-camp should keep guard over him. They did not relish the thoughts of this, persuading themselves, they would be degraded, by obeying the orders. The day following therefore, at a general review of the force, Pedro Mena, in the name of the whole, came forward, and, with very little ceremony, intimated that they would not keep guard, as it was the duty of the privates. The Colonel reprehended them sharply, suspended them, and struck them out of the list of aids-de-camp of the General. This punishment for their insolence, though fully merited, exasperated them to such a degree, that they set fire to their tents, and had nearly burnt all the effects belonging to his Majesty. The principal perpetrators of this crime, were Pedro de Mena, and Terresan, who were executed the following day, and by this act, the subordination of the rest was secured.

The ship Capitana, was by this time prepared, for her voyage to New Spain. Her commander was Phelipe de Salcedo, grandson of the General; and there went in her, the friars Andres de Urdaneta, to conduct her to New Spain, and Martin de Aguirre, to solicit assistance for the conversion of these islanders. They sailed from Zebu on the 1st of June, 1565, and reaching the 36th degree of latitude, in search of the north-west winds, they directed their course to Puerto de la Natividad, where they arrived, after a four months voyage; but considering the distance of this port from Mexico, they pushed forwards to Acapulco, which was nearer, and they arrived there on the 30th of October. In Mexico, their arrival occasioned much exultation, as they were considered to be lost, by the accounts which had been given, by the Captain Arellano and the pilot Lope Martin, who, three months before, had arrived at Puerto de la Natividad. The friars Urdaneta and Aguirre went to Madrid, where they met with Arellano, who was soliciting a reward, for the discovery of the track from the Philippines to New Spain. He had persisted in his pretensions, till the arrival of these friars, when he altered his tone; he was put in confinement, and ordered to Mexico, to be from thence sent to Manila, to be punished by Legaspi as his conduct deserved. The Mexicans, however, were of opinion, that he should not be sent to Manila, until the death of Legaspi was ascertained. The friars Urdaneta and Aguirre, having favourably completed their mission, embarked for Mexico, where Urdaneta died on the 3d of June, 1568, in the 70th year of his age.

CHAPTER V.

ANNO DOM. 1565.

Of the complete Conquest of the Island of Zebu, and of some Towns in other Islands.

The day following that, on which the Capitana sailed, a Moor of Borneo, called Cid Hamal, established in this island, arrived in our camp. He recommended it to the General, to invite Tupas to a conference; and upon this being done, he accordingly presented himself a second time, with some of the chief men of the island, and the conference terminated, in their resolution to preserve a good understanding with the Spaniards. They paid homage to the king of Spain, promising, that the squadron should be supplied with provisions, at the price usual among themselves, and granting land, and every means of founding a Spanish city, with fortifications for its defence. Amity thus restored, the Indians began to re-build their town, and a very short time, exhibited the pleasing sight, of the individuals of two different nations, establishing themselves at a little distance from each other.

The Zebuans lost all apprehensions of the Spaniards, and came to their town to sell fruit, goats, and provisions. Among the least reserved was Tupas, who, under the pretext of accompanying other chiefs, visited the General, making him presents; and so contrived that his women should visit him likewise, dressing themselves in rich clothes, with ear-rings and bracelets of gold on the feet and arms, and accompanied by a great concourse of men and women; which visit was not ill received, the General always treating them handsomely. Tupas likewise, gave Legaspi his niece, who was a widow, and other women to attend him. The General directed them to be instructed in the Christian doctrine, and they embraced our religion, and were baptized. The niece of Tupas, had the name of Isabel given her, in memory of the deceased lady of the General, whose name this was, and in a little time she was married to Maestre Andrea, an officer of the squadron.

The provisions which they had in the island of Zebu, were not sufficient for the Indians and their numerous guests; in consequence of which, Legaspi directed Tupas, to send two chiefs to the island of Panay, to purchase rice. Whilst these men were on their mission, the Spaniards sailed, in vessels which they had constructed at Zebu, on an expedition against some towns, belonging to the enemies of the Zebuans, and were enabled to send some rice to those in the camp. The Moors likewise of the island of Luçon, who came for commercial purposes to Zebu, sold them two hundred baskets of this grain; but as the return of the two ships which had gone to Panay, was still delayed beyond the expected time, Legaspi was compelled to put every man on an allowance, which produced great discontent among the people, and some even adopted the resolution of escaping with the patache San Juan, with the intention of lying in wait behind the islands, to rob the small barks that came there for commerce, and with their spoils to retire to France. The authors of this conspiracy were Pablo Hernandez and Juan Maria Venecianos; and they were joined in it by the pilot Francis Pierres Plin, Jorge el Griego, Maestre Andrea, the husband of Tupas's niece, Geronimo Foxa, and some foreigners. They fixed on the 26th of November, 1565, for their undertaking, intending previously to endeavour to disable all the ships, in order that they might not be pursued. It pleased Heaven to retard their scheme one day beyond the time fixed, and Juan Maria

Venecianos repenting of his treason, discovered the conspiracy to Colonel Matheo del Sauz. The conspirators were immediately all apprehended, except Pablo Hernandez, who escaped into the country among the Indians. The whole underwent an examination, and Legaspi ordered that Francis Pierres Plin, and Jorge el Griego, should be hanged by break of day. It was his intention to have followed up the punishment of the conspirators, and he was proceeding to hang Maestre Andrea. The clergy, however, entreated him to pardon him, on account of his near relationship to Tupas, to which he assented. Pablo Hernandez, pressed by hunger, was compelled to deliver himself up, and as he was the ringleader, he was executed in the middle of the day by proclamation, and his head placed on a pole, as a warning to others. A pardon was granted to all the rest in the name of the King, and by this due mixture of severity and lenity, the minds of the General and the friars were tranquillized.

Famine, at this time, was likely to be the lot of the Spaniards, as the chiefs who had been sent to Panay had not appeared; and as six more paraos had been despatched for the same purpose, it was apprehended that they had entered into a combination with the first, to reduce the Spaniards by famine. In this situation, Captain Martin de Goite set sail, with the intention of taking by force, from the enemies of the Zebuans, as much provision as could be procured, and executed his plan with so much success, that by Christmas he sent to the camp a small vessel laden with borona (bread made of Indian corn and millet). This proved the most acceptable new year's gift, which could have been offered under their circumstances; by degrees provisions became more plentiful, and the people began to revive, and forget

G 2

the famine they had endured. The chiefs now made their appearance from Panay with the rice, but they assigned little of it to the Spaniards, and the largest quantity to the Indians.

The General was well aware of the treachery of the Zebuans, of the little faith to be placed in them, and their doubtful intentions; but he dissembled his sentiments, as they were necessary to his views, and our camp was tolerably well supplied. By the expeditions, which Martin de Goite and others made round the adjacent islands, it was discovered that some of the towns courted the friendship of the Spaniards, while others planned their destruction by famine, for which purpose all the provisions were conveyed to the mountains. The Moors of Luzon, however, found it their interest to bring sufficient rice to Zebu, and Legaspi, who did not wish to see a recurrence of the same danger as had happened, sent the Colonel in search of provisions to the neighbouring islands; but here he encountered another inconvenience, in leaving too small a force for the defence of Zebu; the consequence of which was, that a plot was formed to seize a vessel belonging to the Moors of Luzon, at that time trading at Zebu, to murder all on board, and escape with the vessel to the Moluccas, where the Portuguese would willingly receive them. Juan Nunes de Carrion, and Miguel Gomez Cavecillas, were executed for this piece of treason, after due repentance of their villainy. Captain Martin de Goite, with the provisions he forwarded, at length sent information, that many nations were desirous of becoming vassals of the King of Spain, and the Colonel soon after arrived with above one thousand fanegas of rice, after having stopt at the islands of Mindanao, Negros, and Panay, where he ransomed a Mexican Indian, who had been in the squadron of Villalobos, and had been taken prisoner. Captain Juan de la

Jela, who had likewise gone out in search of provisions, had the good fortune to discover the ship San Geronimo, which he conducted to Zebu; a circumstance which filled every one with joy, mingled with regret, at the thoughts of the tragic scenes which had been acted on board that ship.

The Royal Audience of Mexico had despatched the ship San Geronimo from Acapulco to relieve those at Zebu, and to advertise them of the arrival of the Capitana at that port. They sent as captain of the ship Pedro Sanchez Pericon; as second in command, Juan Ortez de Mosquera, and as pilot the mulatto Lope Martin, who was sent for the express purpose of being punished by Legaspi, for having separated, intentionally, from the squadron in the patache San Lucas. Pericon and Mosquera had been, before the commencement of the voyage, inimical to each other, and in its progress their mutual antipathy was augmented. The pilot, Martin, dreading the idea of being confronted with Legaspi, entered into a plot with Mosquera, and they gained over to their party most of the crew, among whom was Philip de Ocampo, a brave man, but of the worst character. Thinking their strength sufficient, they commenced their operations by being insolent to the commander, and one night they killed a horse which he had brought in the galleon. The friends of Pericon conjured him to be on his guard, as they concluded that those who had begun by killing the horse, would end in murdering him, if he was not sufficiently vigilant. But Pericon's confidence was too great, and he slighted the advice of his friends. The conspirators by this forbearance increasing every day in boldness, at last resolved to put in practice their diabolical design of murdering the commander, and getting possession of the vessel; accordingly one night, after having placed guards on those of the crew whom they could not confide in, Mosquera entered the captain's bedroom, accompanied by two seamen, one of the name of Bartolome de Lara, and the other Morales, and ordered them to stab Captain Pericon and his son, a young man about twenty-five years of age, who had a sub-command in the ship. They effected their purpose, and threw the bodies overboard; and placing some chests on the deck for the accommodation of the people, Mosquera thus harangued them: "Gentlemen, let us recommend to Heaven the souls of Captain Pericon and his son; they came by their death for reasons which, when we arrive at Zebu, shall be given to General Legaspi; every thing shall remain unaltered, and I, as a good subject of his Majesty, will conduct the ship to that island."

Many days had not elapsed before Mosquera and the pilot quarrelled; it was a difficult task for the latter to reconcile himself to his situation, and put on the mask of friendship to the former. He whispered to Mosquera in confidence, that the people were much irritated at the murders which had been committed, and among other things, he proposed to tranquillize them, by putting in irons some person who had been concerned in the affair, and afterwards to discharge him, under the authority of a notarial process, drawn up for that purpose, delaring his innocence. This appearing a plausible measure enough, Mosquera, with this view, foolishly convened the ship's company, and the pilot seized upon him, and put him in confinement. The day following he ordered breakfast, of which Mosquera partook in his irons, and when finished, he requested the pilot would set him at liberty, as there had been time sufficient allowed for the ceremony. The views of the mulatto, however, were very different; he ordered him to be hung at the yard-arm, without giving him time to confess, observing, that Divine Providence had ordered he should die without partaking the sacrament, as had been the case with the two whom he had murdered. The mulatto now remaining captain of the ship, Philip de Ocampo, who was his favourite, made a speech to his companions, telling them, "That Captain Lope Martin did not intend going to Zebu; that those who were desirous of accompanying him, should go to a part of the world where all might acquire great riches, but that those who were of a different opinion, should be set on shore on an island in the immediate neighbourhood of Zebu, from whence they might easily reach Legaspi." All were silent, and nothing was done till they arrived at the islands of Barbudos; when Lope Martin landing on one which was desolate, gave out that it was necessary to careen the ship there, but his real intention was to leave most of his companions on this island, exposed to famine.

He was not, however, able sufficiently

to conceal his intentions. The Friar Capellan, a venerable priest, suspected him, and consulted with Juan de Vivero on some means of averting this blow. Rodrigo de Angle, the mate of the ship, a man of approved courage, determined to appeal to his Majesty, if it cost him his life, broke the matter to others, and eventually drew to his party Bartholome de Lara, by promising to make him captain of the ship, although he had no such intention. Rodrigo finding he had gained most of the crew on board to his side, weighed anchor, and hallooed to those on shore, that all the true and faithful vassals of his Majesty might embark immediately, and that the ship belonged to the King. By this means all were received on board but Lope Martin and Philip de Ocampo, and about twenty-five others, among whom were some loyalists, who were unable to reach the ship in time.

Bartholome de Lara, disappointed in

his expectations of being made captain of the ship, began to form a party, and was joined more from necessity than otherwise by Hernando de Morales, his accomplice in the murder of Pericon and his son; but the new captain contrived means to try and hang them, after which the crew remained free from further molestation, and they arrived at Zebu. The General Legaspi, to deter others, hanged the notary Juan de Zaldivar, for being accessary to the aforesaid murder. He rewarded Rodrigo del Angle, Garnica, and Juan Enriquez, with all the loyalists, and granted a pardon, in the name of the King, to all those who had acted any subordinate part in this transaction.

The Colonel, at this time, had gone to ratify a treaty of peace with some of the towns, and falling in with a small Portuguese galleon of superior force, which bore down upon his patache, he was compelled to escape as well as he could. About the same time, two Portuguese vessels having appeared off Zebu, Legaspi ordered them to be acknowledged as friends, and invited into the harbour, but they excused themselves, and prosecuted their route. These proved afterwards to be ships belonging to the squadron of Pereyra, which was coming against the Spaniards, but being dispersed by storms, they could not pursue their first intentions. The General fortified his camp, and entertaining no fears of the Portuguese, he despatched Martin de Goite on an amicable treaty with some adjacent towns, and to receive the tribute of those who had already submitted. He likewise sent the Colonel to Mindanao, for the purchase of cinnamon, to be shipped to New Spain. This expedition was unfortunate in the death of this great man, who was a severe loss to the Spaniards. He caught a fever, and being in great danger, he told Morones, his second in command, and to whom he entrusted the ship before he died, that he suspected an intention of mutiny among the crew; the object of which was, to go off with the patache, because they had not been allowed to purchase cinnamon for themselves, and which being the only valuable object for which the voyage was undertaken, belonged to the King, as being the first purchase made of that article. Legaspi paid him the usual funeral honours in Zebu, and punished those who were found to be concerned in this mutiny. He likewise named as his successor Martin de Goite. The General sent Morones to Caraga, and Pedro de Herrera to Leyte, for tar, for careening the ships. The Indians of this island are excellent porters and labourers, and our soldiers had such confidence in them, that leaving their arms, and relying on their friendship, they received the tar in an unguarded manner. This, however, in the end, cost them dear, as on a sudden they found themselves surrounded in an ambuscade, by eight or ten Indians to one Spaniard; and Matheo Sanchez Gaditano not being able to extricate them, the Indians murdered all but one Spaniard, who escaped to relate the news of this tragedy. Whilst this was passing up the country, others came down to plunder the ship, who finding our people in unsuspecting security, possessed themselves of their arms, and destroyed every thing they could not take away.

On the 10th of June, 1567, there arrived at Zebu two Portuguese caracoas, with letters from Captain Pereyra to Miguel Lopez de Legaspi, in which he observed, that he supposed they were the Spaniards who had taken refuge in Zebu, in consequence of bad weather, and were unable to return to New Spain, as had happened to those of the other Spanish squadrons which had navigated those seas; and on this supposition he invited them to the Moluccas, where he promised to receive them with every degree of friendship, and furnish them with proper necessaries to prosecute their voyage.

Such were the contents of his letter on the occasion, but some invalid Spaniards who came with the messenger, affirmed that Pereyra had been despatched by the Viceroy of India to drive the Spaniards out of Zebu, and not being able last year to effect it, in consequence of the storms they had encountered, they had remained in Tidore with the intention of completing it this year. Our General, aware of the snare which Pereyra was laying for him, answered this specious letter with corresponding dissimulation, and that he had given notice to his court of the capture of these islands, and was in daily expectation of hearing from his sovereign. Surrounded by these interruptions and difficulties, the

General sent to Acapulco the patache San Lucas, Captain Juan de la Isla, requesting such assistance as might prevent the threatened suspension of their intercourse with New Spain, and which appeared highly probable. The Augustine friars sent, on this occasion, Friar Pedro de Gamboa to solicit some additional aid for the conversion of these infidels, who had already begun to be baptized, and which, they urged, would securely establish the authority of the Spaniards in the Philippines, but the friar never arrived, having died on the voyage.

On the 20th of August, this year, Philip de Salcedo arrived with two ships, and accompanied by his brother Juan de Salcedo, who had been of great use in the first conquest of these islands. The General was rejoiced at the arrival of such considerable relief, at a period when he had reason to think Pereyra intended to attack

Zebu. When Legaspi saw, however, that the Portuguese did not make their appearance as he expected, he despatched his grandson, Philip de Salcedo, to Acapulco, with directions to go by the route of the Ladrone Islands, where he was shipwrecked ; but, all the people being saved, he built another vessel, and returned to Zebu in such happy time, that he made up for his disappointment, by the importance of his appearance, at the period of Pereyra's arrival, on the 30th of September 1568, with as quadron of three galleons, two galeots, three fustas, and twenty smaller vessels. Every thing, however, on this occasion, indicated perfect amity ; the Generals visited reciprocally, and held meetings, to ascertain whether these islands were in the line of demarcation of Spain, or not, with the view of avoiding hostilities. Pereyra, by an artful line of conduct, protracted these discussions, in order to gain time, if possible, by stratagem, to get possession of the port and of our camp, as he found it could not be effected by force. Disappointed, however, in his views, he returned on Christmas-eve to the Moluccas, having been dismissed with great civility by Legaspi.

CHAPTER VI.

ANNO DOM. 1569 to 1571.

Of the Conquest of Manila.

THE supply of provisions having been very short, in consequence of the Portuguese, in some measure, blockading the port, the General, to guard against being exposed to the same danger a second time, determined to change his position, and establish himself in a more fertile country than that he then occupied. He ordered the camp to be immediately removed to the island of Panay: with this commission he charged his grandson, Philip de Salcedo, who was very cordially received by the natives, because he had formerly assisted them against their enemies, and enabled them to make many prisoners. Captain Luis de la Haya was ordered to go with his detachment, to the river Araut in the same island; Captain Andres de Ybarra to the island of Masbate; and the Colonel was ordered to remain in Zebu. In the interim the camp was established in Panay, and the patache San Lucas remained at Zebu, preparing to depart for New Spain. Juan de Salcedo ordered his brother Philip to Panay with another vessel, which conveyed the books and effects of his grandfather, all of which were lost in a storm; which loss, although he felt it severely, Legaspi bore with exemplary patience and fortitude.

Philip de Salcedo having loaded the patache San Lucas, sailed from Zebu, and, in a few days after her departure, fell in with the San Juan, which had sailed from Acapulco, and was commanded by Captain Juan Lopez de Aguirre; Salcedo returned with her to Zebu, and, on the 10th of July, sailed a second time on his voyage. By the San Juan the Augustine fathers had sent Friar Herrera, having appointed him a provincial, or clerical head of a province, which was the first they had established in the Philippines. Their intention was by this appointment, to increase the importance of the religious orders, and induce higher respect from the new converts; the effect, accordingly, was the addition of many to the number, stimulated too, by the example of Tupas and his son: Legaspi stood godfather to Tupas, who was christened Philip, in compliment to the King of Spain; and his son was christened Charles, and had, as his godfather, Juan de Salcedo. The feasts which were held on the day these two new Christians were baptized, contributed, at the same time, to the conversion of many others. This was a measure of great expediency, although the duty of the fathers became necessarily so much more enlarged. It was determined that a friar, whose name was Juan Alba, should be sent to attempt the conversion of the isle of Masbate; and another, by the name of Alonzo Ximenes, to the river Araut, in the island of Panay, where he made many converts. Friar Martin de Rada remained in Zebu, and the rest of the clergy accompanied the General in the conquest of Manila.

The General Legaspi arrived at Panay, accompanied by the Colonel, who, however, immediately returned to his command at Zebu, together with his wife, who had just arrived from New Spain with Captain Juan Lopez de Aguirre, in the ship San Juan. Legaspi was received by the natives of Panay with every demonstration of joy, and they appeared more sincere in their professions than those of Zebu. He constructed, with all expedition, some works, to enable him to resist the attempts of the squadron of Pereyra, and check the proceedings of a swarm of pirates, which had issued from Jolo and Borneo in twenty vessels, called *vireyes*, and had captured a Spanish vessel, with the crew. The Colonel attacked these pirates with nine *proas*: he took four *vireyes*, and would have taken the whole, had not seven of his vessels been too much astern. Having forwarded the account of this engagement to the General, he was now at liberty to assist the inhabitants of Aclan, who had sustained considerable injury from the pirates of Mindoro. In the month of January, 1570, Juan de Salcedo sailed on this expedition with thirty Spaniards and many friendly Indians. He entered the town of Mamburao, and, having made himself master of it, compelled the inhabitants to ransom themselves with gold; after which he proceeded to the isle of Lucban, where the pirates of Mindoro had taken refuge, and had protected themselves by some indifferent works; he, with ease, forced their intrenchments, attacked them with fire-arms, and, as they were unable to resist this mode of warfare, they agreed to ransom themselves with gold, as the inhabitants of Mamburao had done. Salcedo divided the spoil among his soldiers and the Indians, and returned to Panay, to give an account of this expedition.

The General, who was determined above all things on the conquest of Manila, named the Colonel as commandant, and sent with him his grandson, Juan de Salcedo, with an hundred and twenty Spaniards, and many friendly Indians, to accomplish it. They sailed from Panay the beginning of May 1570. The Colonel went directly against Manila, but Juan de Salcedo turned aside to the country about the lake of Bombon, which is now called the Province of Batangas, to treat with the natives. He sent the usual peace-offerings, but they answered him with their arms. He engaged them, and would have succeeded, but received so severe a wound in his leg from an arrow, that he was compelled to abandon his enterprise, and follow the Colonel to Manila. The Colonel made terms with the Rajah, who was a good old man, and whom history calls Raxa Matanda, that is, the old Rajah; he had a nephew of the name of Raxa Soliman, who, likewise, made terms with the Colonel; but little dependence could be placed on him, as he evidently was no friend to the Spaniards, and had, as it was supposed, secreted provisions. He was accused, likewise, of exciting the Indians to murder the Spaniards, while on shore, which obliged our people to behave with great circumspection toward them. One day Raxa Soliman even ordered his men to fire upon our shipping, and, after having done us considerable damage, he embarked on board a large junk, and left the river, firing at us as he passed[17]. The Colonel instantly landed, leaving Juan de Salcedo in charge of the ships, and, with eighty men, stormed the fort which the Indians had at the mouth of the river, and where at present stands the fort of Santiago. He ordered his soldiers to attack the guns, and they were so fortunate in their attack, as in their first onset to kill the principal artillery officer, who appeared to be an European, as he was seen to cross himself before he died [18]; the remainder, were by the vigour of the assault, compelled to fly towards the town, which they burnt in their retreat, that the Spaniards might not profit by their success. Among other things, a foundery for cannon was destroyed, and it was supposed they had thrown many pieces of artillery into the sea, as only twelve, and a few falconets (a piece so called), were found in the place. The old Rajah was not a party in this disturbance, as neither he nor any of his people were engaged; and his fidelity was proved, by his having displayed from his house a white flag, during the time the action lasted. The Colonel, fearing that if he remained longer, he should encounter the south-west monsoon, and be unable to return, retired immediately to Cavite, to do the needful repairs to his ships, and in two days sailed for Panay.

On the 23d of June of this year, Captain Juan de la Isla arrived with three vessels, in which came the Friar Perrera with two other religious, viz. Friar Diego Orduñez, and Friar Diego de Espinar, who came to labour in this new vineyard. Despatches were brought by them from his Majesty, by which Miguel Lopez de Legaspi was constituted President of the islands of the Ladrones, and he was recommended to settle the Philippines; at the same time his Majesty bestowed portions of lands, with their inhabitants, on all who might be engaged in the conquest. With a view to put these orders in execution, Legaspi first despatched from Panay, the same Captain Juan de la Isla, with two ships to Acapulco, and sailed for Zebu, where he ordered it to be proclaimed, that he intended to erect the town which had been built into a city, and to give every encouragement to increase the population, directing those who wished to settle in it to go before the notary, to be enrolled by five hundreds. On New Year's day, 1571, he named two ordinary alcaldes, six regidores, a notary, and two alguazils, who immediately took the customary oath on entering their office, and he strictly enjoined them the discharge of their respective duties. He likewise directed that the town, which had till then been called San Miguel, should be named the City del Santissimo Nombre de Jesus, in memory of the discovery of the sacred child, as before related. He settled the manner, in which rewards should be distributed among the tributary Indians, who were in the neighbourhood of the city, and left them under the care of the treasurer, Guido de Labezares, in order that he might have the opportunity of finishing a stone fort, which he had ordered to be constructed. All these and many subordinate objects, being attained by the end of January, he returned to Panay, to attempt from thence the conquest of Manila.

Immediately after the President arrived at Panay, the Colonel, attended by all the officers and soldiers, joined him, leaving in Masbate the Padre Alba with six men, and in Dumangas Padre Ximenes, in charge of the new conquests. The Padre Herrera, with other religious, accompanied the General in his expedition against Manila, on which he sailed the 15th of April; and in the island of Lutaga he reviewed his force, and found they amounted to two hundred and eighty soldiers, consisting partly of his own people, of those of the Colonel, of Captains Andres de Ybarra, Luis de la Haya, and Juan de Salcedo. He passed by the island of Mindoro, and settled the tribute which the natives were to pay to the King of Spain. Here he had the opportunity of saving a Chinese vessel called a Sampan, from foundering; and he received the crew, with that kindness and warmth of feeling, so natural to the Spaniards.

The Chinese acknowledged the kindness of the Spaniards, and formed a friendly connection with them. The President continued his voyage, and entered Cavite, where he waited the arrival of those who had fallen astern; meantime he treated with the natives of the place, and received them as vassals of the King of Spain. Two days after he arrived, he entered with all his squadron into the river of Manila. The Indians, thinking the Spaniards had returned, to punish them for the resistance they had made to the Colonel, set fire to the town, and with their effects fled to Tondo. The President sent the Colonel to bring them to terms, who, arriving at their camp, gave them to understand, by means of an interpreter, that the Spaniards had not come with the intention of doing them any injury. On learning this, some began to quench the flames, and others went in search of the old Rajah; and Lacandola, the chief of Tondo, immediately went with others to wait on Legaspi. He received them with a smiling countenance, and told them that he came as a friend, provided they acknowledged the King of Spain, as their king and natural lord and master, who would receive them under his protection, and relieve their distresses. The principal motive, he said, which induced his Majesty to send him there, was to propagate the true worship of one all powerful God; that he had brought several sacred characters with him for that purpose, and shewing them Padre Herrera, said that he was the principal of those, who were to be their teachers. They promised to become vassals of the King of Spain, and hear the law which they were to be taught; he hinted to them that he did not see Rajah

Soliman with them: they replied, that he dared not appear after what had happened with the Colonel on the first expedition; but if he would pardon him, he would immediately appear, and promise obedience, as the rest had done. The General not only promised to pardon him, but sent him a message to that effect, without, however, being able to remove his apprehensions at that time.

But on the 18th of May, Rajah Soliman arrived, accompanied by his uncle Rajah Matanda and Lacandola, making many apologies for what had passed. The General pardoned and received him as a vassal of his Majesty, and as such he was registered by the notary, Hernando Riguel. Legaspi immediately commenced his arrangements for founding a new city, and directed the Indians to finish the fort they had begun in the mouth of the river. Behind this he erected a large building, which served as a palace, with a church and convent for the religious, and an hundred and twenty smaller houses for the remainder of the Spaniards, intending this city to be the seat of government, both spiritual and temporal, of the islands. The whole of this, the Indians engaged to accomplish with great despatch, but it was found necessary, to employ the Spaniards to assist them in it. A good understanding being thus established, between the natives of Manila and Tondo and the Spaniards, Manila was taken possession of on the day following, the 19th of May, 1571, when, in a temporary church, the feast of the blessed Virgin Mary was celebrated, who, from that circumstance, was named the patroness of the new city.

The peace which Rajah Soliman and Lacandola had made, was, on their part, by no means sincere, for the Indians of Macabebe and Hagonoy, appearing at the mouth of the harbour of Bancusay, with forty caracoas (an Indian vessel), proceeded to the house of Lacandola. These men jeered at and reproached the Indians, for submitting with such readiness, to such an insignificant number of Spaniards, promising, if they were disposed to shake off the yoke, that they should be assisted from Tondo and the neighbouring country, and not leave one Spaniard alive. The President, supposing those Indians who had arrived, had come to solicit peace, sent two Spaniards to assure them that they might present themselves to him without fear. The chief of the Indians, after listening to these ambassadors, leaped on his feet, and drawing and flourishing his cimeter, he said, "The sun gave me life, and I must not be disgraced in the eyes of my women, who would detest me, if they thought I was capable, of being on friendly terms with the Spaniards." With this speech he quitted the house, without waiting to go down by the ladder, for, with great boldness, he

I 2

leaped out of the window into his caracoa, calling out to the Spaniards, "I expect you in the bay of Bancusay." Legaspi determined upon punishing such conduct, and sent against him the Colonel Martin de Goite with eighty Spaniards, in some newly constructed small vessels. The Indian chief was true to his word, and waited for them where he had said, with his squadron. The battle began, and he fought with great valour; but, in a short time, being killed by a musket shot, the rest dismayed, fled with great precipitation; our people pursued, and made many prisoners, among whom were the son of Lacandola, and his nephew, by which his deceit and dissimulation were sufficiently manifest; the President, however, sent them home, without the punishment they merited for their treason. After this engagement, the natives became so much afraid of the Spaniards, that many chiefs came to Manila begging peace, and offering to become vassals of the king of Spain. By this time, the works which had been ordered in Manila were considerably advanced, and, on the day of St. John the Baptist, the President, Miguel Lopez de Legaspi, founded the city as the metropolis of the Philippine Islands, appointing two ordinary alcaldes, twelve regidores, an alguazil mayor, and a notary, who all took the customary oaths, to discharge the duties of their respective offices with justice. This ceremony took place while Philip II. was King of Spain, and Pius V. was in the fifth year of his pontificate, the first governor being the President, Miguel Lopez de Legaspi. The public square was now marked out, with the situation of the convent of San Augustine, and the subordinate arrangements were left to the magistracy. Legaspi ordered the city to be called Manila, of which his Majesty approved, giving it a coat of arms. This city is placed in fourteen degrees and a half of north latitude, and is thought to be the antipodes of the river Saint Ann, in Brazil, which is in the same latitude in the opposite tropic of Capricorn.

CHAPTER VII.

ANNO DOMINI, 1571.

Of the Government of Miguel Lopez de Legaspi.

MANILA being founded, and most of the towns of the surrounding district, in amity with the Spaniards, the Governor sent the Colonel to Pampanga, to reduce that province to the Spanish yoke, but he had no sooner arrived at the river Betis, on his way thither, than he was compelled to return, without being able to reduce either the town of Betis or that of Lubao; for it appeared that Rajah Soliman and Lacandola, who had gone with him to serve as interpreters between the Indians and him, had conducted themselves treacherously. This fully appeared by Lacandola leaving the Colonel, and returning to Manila without leave, for which the Governor ordered him to be put in irons, and, to increase his punishment, told his relations that he would not let him at liberty but at the Colonel's request; even then he did not accede to it without confiscating all his artillery, consisting of fifteen pieces of cannon, large and small. About this time Rajah Matanda fell sick, and requesting to be baptized, a clergyman of the name of Juan de Vivero administered this sacrament to him by the name of Philip: he died of his disorder, and was buried with great solemnity. On the 17th of July, Don Diego Legaspi, a nephew of the Governor, arrived; he was sent by Captain Juan de Aguirre to the aid of his uncle, having a short time before come to Panay with two ships, which the Viceroy of Mexico had sent to these islands as a reinforcement. The Governor ordered the Colonel to proceed to Panay, and despatch these ships to

Manila, and afterwards go to Zebu, and bring his family to the capital. Whilst the Colonel was executing this commission, Juan de Salcedo was sent to reduce the people of Cainta and Taytay, two small towns high up the river Pasig, which had refused to acknowledge the Spanish authority, and had strengthened their position by some fortifications covering their towns. He carried Cainta by assault, with the loss of only two killed and five wounded, but with great slaughter on the part of the Indians, upon hearing which, the inhabitants of Taytay immediately surrendered. He afterwards marched to a town on the borders of the lake *Bay*, and of the same name, and summoned the inhabitants, but they answered him with their arms in their hands. He had with him Padre Friar Alonso de Albarado, who had accompanied Ruy Lopez de Villalobos in his expedition; had returned a second time to Mexico; and again had accompanied the other five religious, of the order of San Augustine, to Manila. This venerable person the Colonel sent, to assure the Indians, that he did not wish to employ his arms against them, and that he had commissioned the Padre Friar Alonso, to accommodate matters, requesting them immediately to deliver up their town of Bay. This in the end was acceded to, and was followed, by the submission of many small towns, on the borders of the lake. Juan de Salcedo went further up the country behind them, and found the people of Mahayhay, fortified by nature so securely on a hill, that they could defend themselves against a great force, with no difficulty, by rolling down immense stones. Having, however, reconnoitred it, he perceived a path less rugged than the rest, and where they seemed more negligent. By this path he surmounted the difficulty, and appeared above them, when they were seized with such a panic, that they fled precipitately, without making any resistance. For two days more, Juan de Salcedo was detained in this part of the country, passing through the villages, which, however, he found deserted, the inhabitants having taken refuge in the mountains. He in consequence returned to Bay, where he had left most of his people. It was understood, that in the country of the Camarines, there was a town called Paracale, where there were mines of gold. He sent back to Manila Padre Albarado, and some of the Spaniards; and having a few soldiers only, he encountered a great many difficulties, in undertaking the conquest of this town. Many days having elapsed, without hearing from them at Manila, the Governor despatched Major Antonio Hurtado in search of them, and he found Juan de Salcedo in Paracale, with all his people, very much weakened, in consequence of the hardships they had been exposed to, and the sickness with which they had been attacked. Salcedo returned with Hurtado to Manila, on which occasion there were great rejóicings, as he had been supposed dead, and the loss of a man so much loved and respected would have been severely felt.

About this time the Colonel returned from Zebu, having first subdued the province of Pampanga. The Governor now apportioned the conquered districts and towns, among the respective officers, who had so well earned that reward, reserving to his Majesty the usual tribute only. He directed, that the Indians should pay a moderate rent, to those new proprietors of land, and the Spaniards were enjoined, not to exact any thing above the rent so settled. In a little time it was discovered, that the Indians would not pay the tribute; and that the Spanish proprietors, had been guilty of many vexatious acts against them, which had produced revolts in various places. In Bohol, Panay, and in Marinduque, the Indians had killed several Spanish factors and soldiers. To prevent these disturbances from spreading, the Governor sent Captain Luis de la Haya, to examine into the matter, and to punish the aggressors. He executed his commission with such prudence, that, without exasperating the Indians, he chastised the murderers, and left the towns in complete subordination.

At the beginning of the year 1572, there arrived, with a great deal of rich merchandize, those Chinese whom the Spaniards had saved from shipwreck, in the island of Mindoro, together with many others of that nation, who brought damasks, satins, taffeties, silks, porcelain, and other things, with which the foundation of a lucrative commerce with Acapulco was laid. These Chinese, whom we call Sangleyes, from two Chinese words, *hiang*, *lay*, which signifies travelling merchants, continue to this day the commerce with Manila, and many have settled in these islands, where, however, they have frequently been troublesome, as will be seen in the sequel. About the time these merchants arrived, the Augustine friars intended to hold their second provincial chapter, and the first which had been celebrated at Manila; and at this it was determined, to send some of their order to China, to establish a religious intercourse between the two nations. The Governor agreed to this, and was desirous, at the same time, to send an embassy to the Emperor; but the Chinese would not agree to take it to China. The Friar Alvarado, however, who was the most desirous of the undertaking, began to study the language, that he might be able to convert and baptize the Chinese merchants, who seemed disposed to settle in Manila; this plan he had adopted in Tondo, where he had administered the sacrament to numbers. In this provincial chapter it was agreed, that Padre Herrera should be sent a second time to Mexico, in order to bring more clerical aid to this province; they likewise chose as provincial, the Padre Friar Martin de Rada, and elected a capitular of the convent of Manila; they established clergy in Zebu, Masbate, Otong, Mindoro, Tondo, Calumpit, and Lubao. Soon after this, convents were founded in the districts of Taal, Bay, and Pasig, and many visitations were made, by which it was ascertained, that the number of the clergy increased so much, that it became necessary, to separate the parish priests from the friars.

The greater part of this quarter of the island, being reduced to complete obedience, to the King of Spain, and nothing being known of the northern part of it, Juan de Salcedo offered to make the discovery, at his own risk. He collected men and ships, the Governor allowing him forty-five soldiers, with necessary ammunition. He sailed from Manila on the 20th of May, 1572; on the third day, he arrived at Cape Bolinao, in the province of Zambales, where he found a Chinese junk or sampan, and a party of Chinese, who had got possession of a chief and some Indians, with an intent to carry them to China. Juan de Salcedo re-took them from the Chinese, and gave them their liberty, which action so gratified the feelings of the natives, that they became immediately vassals of the King of Spain, and solicited to be placed on the same footing, as the people of the other districts. Passing from thence to Pangasinan, he coasted the whole of that province, and that of Ylocos, until he arrived at Cape Boxeador, examining all the ports, bays, and landing places, near which his squadron was able to approach, and it consisted of many, but very small vessels. He was desirous, of preserving a good understanding with the Indians, and most of the towns on the coast, received him in a very friendly manner, and supplied him with provisions, which he stood in need of; but on his entering the rivers and creeks, he found great resistance from the inhabitants of the districts bordering on them. He attacked them on several occasions, putting them to flight with great ease, and sent to them, desiring them to leave the mountains, with a promise of his friendship. Some, however, not relying on the promises of the Spaniards, could not divest themselves of their apprehensions, while others readily came down, submitted, and agreed to pay the tribute. In this manner he was proceeding, and had almost subdued these two large provinces[19], intending to pass on to Cagayan; but he was opposed by his own people, who became weary of the expedition. His second in command, Antonio Hurtado, proposed that he should go on, and prosecute his original plan, but Juan de Salcedo, although he desired it much, thought it better to accede to the representations of his soldiers, and they returned by the same route, confirming in their obedience the towns which had submitted. On his arrival at Bigan, the natives received him with so much cordiality, that he prudently determined on the step of founding there a Spanish city, for the purpose of controuling the neighbouring country.

Having, with this view, ordered the natives to cut sufficient timber to build a fort, and accommodations for those who chose to remain, he became desirous of executing the original project, which he had abandoned, of passing on to Cagayan. He left in Bigan his second in command, with twenty-five soldiers, and, with the seventeen that remained, he commenced this arduous undertaking, departing in three vessels on the 24th of July. Having passed Cape Boxeador, he entered a river where he found a mud village of salt-makers; he desired them to call their chiefs, as he wished to be on good terms with them, and after many messages they appeared with their Rajah, who was a very handsome man, and whiter than the rest of the Indians.

Juan de Salcedo came up to him with open arms, intending to embrace him; but the barbarian, unaccustomed to such a mode of salutation, believing that he wanted to catch him, took to his heels and fled, and on no entreaty would he be prevailed on, to leave the mountains. Our people, therefore, hoisted their sails, and arrived at the river of Cagayan. They sailed up this river a considerable way, and found a populous district; but they dared not attempt any hostility against the inhabitants, as they were so few in number in comparison to the natives, and they resolved to return to Manila by that side of the island, in order completely to ascertain the whole extent of Luzon. They proceeded about one hundred leagues, without discovering any population, or any thing but a rocky shore. They coasted it until they arrived at a bay, which Juan de Salcedo thought had been named Amanto, having been there when he went to Paracale. In this, however, he was mistaken, but as that bay was very near, he arrived in a few days at it. Here he went on shore; and travelled on till he came to the towns on the lake, where he embarked on board a small boat with only four rowers. The boat was on the point of foundering during the passage, and the Indians deserting her by swimming away, he would inevitably have been lost, had not a proa, with some friendly Indians, passing by, immediately relieved him. Arriving at Manila, he received the melancholy intelligence of the death of his grandfather, on the 20th of August, 1572, accelerated much by the vexatious and multifarious duties of his office. He was interred in the church of the Augustines, with the magnificence due to his character and station.

By the death of Legaspi, the treasurer, Guido de Labezares became governor *ad interim,* by a decree of the Royal Audience of Mexico, and which decree was found among the papers of the deceased. A few days after Labezares had succeeded to the government, Manila suffered severely from a hurricane, which destroyed almost all the houses, these being built of canes, and drove back the two ships which had been seent to Acapulco, but which, after the storm subsided, sailed again for New Spain, carrying accounts of the death of Legaspi. The new Governor sent Colonel Martin de Goite, to reduce the revolted natives of Ylocos, which was done with little trouble, and he brought away the tribute of the king in gold, compelling them to ransom themselves, for a sum far exceeding that amount. This he was enabled so easily to do, by the exertions of Juan de Salcedo, who, at his own cost, had subdued nearly all this province, and who, as the Colonel represented, ought to be allowed to reap the fruits of his labours; but Guido de Labezares was prejudiced against him, and would not employ him until he was undeceived as to his merits. He then sent him to the conquest of the Camarines, which he effected with ease, and founded near the river of Vicol a Spanish city, calling it Santiago de Libon. He appointed as chief judge Captain Pedro de Chaves, with eighty soldiers. While Juan de Salcedo was making these conquests, the governor *ad interim* was exploring the whole of the Bisayas: he attempted to restrain within proper bounds the avarice of the factors, but it was without effect, as the moment he was gone they returned to their old practices. Meanwhile a ship from Acapulco arrived with three Augustine friars, men who were much required, not only for the purpose, of converting to the Christian religion, the natives of the conquered countries, but likewise to preserve the tranquillity of the different towns, and which could not be effected solely by force of arms.

When the Governor *ad interim* returned

to Manila, he sent an embassy to the Rajah of Borneo, but without effect, as he had no wish to be on terms with the Spaniards. He likewise divided the province of Ylocos between the Colonel and Juan de Salcedo, who had been employed in that expedition. In the beginning of the year 1574, Juan de Salcedo sailed to take possession of his portion; he founded in the district of Bigan the city Fernandina, where he built a house for himself. While he was accomplishing this object, a large squadron of vessels passed by, which had taken a galeot and twenty men he had sent in search of provisions; and presuming that their intention was to attack him, he began to fortify the town, but seeing they prosecuted their route, he took it for granted they were going against Manila; and having collected together all the Spaniards he had in Ylocos, he embarked for the capital to the assistance of the Governor. This was the famous expedition of Limahon, by which Manila was nearly lost, but a short time after its foundation.

Limahon was a pirate of such renown, that the Emperor of China had sent against him three different squadrons, and he was in fact so pressed on all sides by this force, that having captured a Chinese junk coming from Manila, who informed him of the new conquests by the Spaniards, he determined to sail for this country, and be crowned King of these islands, in order to be secure, by this means, from the Emperor's attacks. He arrived at the island of Corregidor, which is in the mouth of the bay, the 29th of November 1574, with sixty-two junks, in which he brought one thousand five hundred women, two thousand soldiers, and a great many seamen, sufficient artillery, muskets, and swords. The Spaniards had no intimation of his arrival at Corregidor, and the same night his second in command, who was a Japanese of the name of Sioco, landed with six hundred men, with which he entered, and attempted to take possession of Manila. In the attempt to land his men he lost three boats, which were swamped by the surf; but he effected his object, without being at all discovered by our people. He first landed at Parañaque, supposing it to be Manila, but soon finding out his mistake, he began his march to it by the beach, his vessels following him, and at day-break he arrived at Manila, where he was discovered by the Indians. They made all haste to the Colonel, who lived close to the royal gate, where the college of St. Joseph now stands, and informed him, that there was an immense body of Moors of Borneo coming by the sea side. The Colonel, however, as he had no reason to conclude, that the Borneans considered themselves, in direct hostility with the Spaniards, gave no credit to it, till he saw the Chinese enter by the gate, close to his house. Three soldiers, who were placed as guards there, attempted to resist them, but they were soon overpowered by multitudes, and one only escaped, severely wounded.

The wife of the Colonel looking out of the window, thought they were Indians come against them, and called out, "Here the dogs come, we are all dead." The Portuguese interpreter, who accompanied Sioco, enraged at this reproachful epithet of the lady, ordered the house to be set on fire. The Colonel, who was ill, immediately on this got up, put on his armour, and unsheathing his sword, leapt out of the window in the midst of his enemies, who received him on their swords, and cut him to pieces. They killed the wife of a common soldier, whom they found in the house, and left for dead Dona Lucia Corral, the wife of the Colonel, but she afterwards recovered from her wounds. Sioco pursuing his march, encountered some Spaniards who were on their way to assist the Governor, and seeing that there were few opposed to him, he formed his men into a half moon, and charged the centre of the Spaniards. The engagement was long doubtful, when eight soldiers being killed, the rest must have shared their fate, had they not been joined by twenty more, under the command of Captain Alonso Velasquez, the aid-de-camp of General Amador de Arriaran, and Gaspar Ramirez, aid-de-camp of the Colonel, who charged the Chinese so furiously, that Sioco was obliged to retire to his boats and join Limahon, who had anchored in Cavite. Sioco justified his ill success in this action, by saying, that the people were tired by their long march along the beach, which excuse Limahon admitted, and determined on another assault on the third day. This affair having happened on St. Andrew's day, the Spaniards attributed it to the intercession of that Saint, that they had not all fallen into the hands of the Chinese, and expressed their gratitude, by choosing him patron of Manila, instituting an annual solemn feast on the occasion. Limahon's delay of the second attack, was the means of saving all, as it gave time to Juan de Salcedo, to join with his force from Ylocos. He arrived in the bay, in the night of the same day of St. Andrew, and understanding that Limahon was in Cavite, he did not attempt to enter there, but landed on the Pampanga side of the bay. The day following, in the evening, he met with two Indians, who had escaped from the engagement, and informed him of all that had happened; he immediately made sail, and entered Manila that night. When he was at the mouth of the river, he ordered the trumpets to be sounded, and placed a great number of lights about his ship, to induce the enemy to believe, the approach of considerable relief to the Spaniards, who saluted him in form, all of which caused great alarm to the Chinese. The Governor *ad interim*, was so pleased with the diligence of Juan de Salcedo, that he appointed him Colonel, in the room of Martin de Goite.

The same night, Limahon weighed anchor from Cavite, and pressed on to Manila, and Sioco disembarked the following morning, after having sworn by an oath to his General, that he would either die in the attempt, or that day be in possession of the house of the Governor. He directed his march to the fort, which our people had constructed of timber, faggots, and barrels of earth, and he divided his troops into three bodies. He ordered one to march down, through the principal street of the city, to the square, where he expected the Spaniards would sally out of the fort, and engage them; and in this expectation, he sent another body, by the side of the river round the fort, and the third, which he commanded himself, he led along the beach. The division which had been ordered down the principal street, arrived in the square, and in order to induce the Spaniards to sally from the fort, they set fire to the houses. Fortunately the Spaniards did not quit the fort, though they saw their houses burning, but contented themselves with playing their artillery upon the Chinese, doing a great deal of mischief. Sioco, finding that it was not possible, to draw the Spaniards from their fortifications, and having lost many of his men, ordered the division that had arrived at the square, to assault the fort, at the same time leading on his own. Such was the multitude of the Chinese, against so few on our part, that the palisade was forced, and they entered through a part, which Ensign Sancho Ortez defended, and in which he was killed, performing prodigies of valour. Immediately the Governor heard of this, he repaired to the fort, attended by the Colonel; they cut their way through the Chinese, and having entered it, repulsed the invaders with great loss. The Chinese, panic struck at this, retiring by degrees towards the shore, the Spaniards followed them close, making great slaughter among them; but, to our great misfortune, our people suddenly abandoned their advantage, at the sight of Limahon's squadron, which had just entered the river, but had not been able hitherto, to take part in the action.

Limahon observing this, ordered his ships off, in order that his men might become desperate, on finding themselves deprived of all protection from him: the contrary effect, however, was produced by it, as they were seized with such a panic, that they could not face their enemies, but formed themselves on the shore, and received the fire of our artillery, which was discharged repeatedly upon them, determined rather to wait death with firmness, than return into the engagement. In this they would have persisted, had not Limahon arrived with four hundred fresh men. As all was not lost, he ordered some of his people to burn a ship and galley, which, with a few other small vessels, were drawn up on the beach, and which, when they had destroyed the houses, they had forgot to burn with the rest, and he made a false attack on the fort, in order to compel the Spaniards to sally out, to hinder the operation. The Colonel guessed his intention: he, however, sallied out with fifty men, against those only who were proceeding to pillage the city, and put them to flight precipitately. Limahon seeing that his plan had not succeeded, having lost many men, and finding that his principal captain, Sioco, had been killed, he embarked his troops, and, under favour of the night, returned to the river Parañaque, where he killed all the Indians, he found assembled in any hostile way, and, before day-break, he set sail, and did not bring to, until he came to the province of Pangasinan; where he entered into an amicable arrangement with the chief, forming an encampment, and fortifying it with a strong palisado on an inlet of the river Lingayen. The Governor was determined to follow him into the province, but he found it necessary first to restore the fortifications of the city, and likewise to quell a sedition of the Indians, who, on this occasion, shewed how little they could be depended upon.

The natives of Manila, whilst the Spaniards were engaging the Chinese, robbed their houses and maltreated their slaves; those of Tondo killed some Sachristans belonging to a convent, and they would have done the same with the clergy, but that they could not have concealed it. Those of the island of Mindoro, however, imprisoned the friars, and took them to the mountains, where they were not bold enough to murder them, till they saw how the action with Limahon would terminate, and how things would be adjusted. Rajah Soliman and Lacandola, the chief of Manila and Tondo, apprehensive that the Governor would punish them for this ill conduct, retired to Navotas, where they fomented a rebellion. In order to quell this the Colonel, accompanied by Friar Marin, set out immediately, and when Lacandola understood they had arrived, he sent to them to request the friar would repair to a station about three leagues distant, where all the chiefs were assembled, and where they were desirous of treating of a reconciliation with the Spaniards. The friar Marin determined to proceed to the station which they mentioned, and there he met all the chiefs, who received him with much joy, but they could not be persuaded to see the Colonel. Lacandola alone abandoned his fears, in consequence of the promise the friar had made him, and left Navotas with an intention to present himself, but he found that Juan de Salcedo had returned, and directed his way to his house. Salcedo encountered two ranks of armed men on the banks of the river, near the house of Lacandola; he boldly went up to them, and took away their lances and arrows; when, Lacandola arriving, he said, "What is the meaning of this? why are these men armed?" The Indian made many excuses, and promised to wait on the Governor the day following, in company with the friar Marin. The Governor admitted the excuses, and presented Lacandola with a silk mantle and a gold chain. Won over by this treatment, Rajah Soliman, in four days, presented himself to the Governor, and the sedition was thus terminated. Captain Rivera subdued the people of Mindoro with the same facility.

The Governor being relieved from the anxiety, which the restlessness of the Indians had occasioned, determined to follow Limahon to Pangasinan. He found, on mustering, that the soldiers in Manila amounted to two hundred, and about two hundred more were scattered through the provinces of Bisayas and Camarines; from

L 2

among these he manned the squadron, with two hundred and fifty Spaniards, and he added one thousand five hundred friendly Indians. On the 22d of March 1575, the Colonel sailed with this armament to Pangasinan, and, on the 29th of the same month, in the night, arrived in the river Lingayen. The day following he sent Captain Pedro de Chaves to take possession of the ships belonging to the corsair, and Captain Gabriel de Rivera to reconnoitre his fortifications. Chaves executed his commission with ease, as the Chinese fled from their ships, the moment he boarded them. Rivera attacked the works, firing upon them, and making a dreadful carnage. Limahon, observing what passed, ordered his men under cover of a grove of date trees, where they might defend themselves more easily. Captain Chaves sent assistance to Rivera, and a most sanguinary engagement commenced. Rivera at last routed the Chinese, compelling them to retire to their fort, which he would have scaled, but, finding the palisade too lofty, he had recourse to the expedient of ordering his men to rush in a body against it, formed as it was of date trees driven into the earth. This they did with such force, that they broke through, opened the gate, and entered the fort. The Chinese then retired within the second palisade, which was the quarter of Limahon. The Spaniards ought to have attacked the inner fort, before the Chinese had recovered from their panic; but their avarice prevailed, and they dispersed themselves through the different houses, which had been built within the first palisade, plundering them, without attempting any thing else. Limahon was not slow in taking advantage of this error of the Spaniards, and, attacking them with four hundred men, he drove them out of the works with great loss, thus paying dearly for the indulgence of their habits of plunder. Ashamed of this defeat, our people returned a second time to the assault, when they retook the first line of works, but being unable to force the inner one, they burnt the houses of the Chinese, and going on board their boats, they retired to where Pedro de Chaves was posted. Here, finding one of the junks unserviceable, she was set fire to, and a retreat of the whole body was made good, to the post where the Colonel was stationed, with the rest of the armament.

Juan de Salcedo, convinced of the difficulty of taking the fort by storm, and desirous of being as sparing as possible, of the lives of his Spaniards, considering the difficulties they had to encounter, determined on attempting to reduce Limahon by fair means. Having in his army a Chinese who had been established in Manila, he ordered him to write to Limahon; but this letter having no effect, he wrote a second to the same purpose. Limahon replied, that he was considered a savage tiger, whom all were desirous of catching; but he assured them, that he should either kill them, or they him. The Chinese, therefore, thus declining every amicable proposal, the Colonel resolved to throw up works near to their works, but at such a distance as to be without the range of the enemy's artillery. Upon his beginning accordingly to pitch his camp, however, a shot was fired which passed close to him, and wounded his aid-de-camp in the leg, affording him a convincing proof that their artillery could reach all over the small island. It was, therefore, deemed necessary to remove the camp to another position, and to blockade the mouth of the river to prevent Limahon from escaping, until the Governor of Manila should determine, whether he would have the works taken by assault, or that, by means of a blockade, the Chinese should be starved into submission. Upon this retreat of the Spaniards, Limahon collected the remaining fragments of the junks, which had been burnt, and with these built some boats within the fort. Four months passed in this manner, when, finding he had no other resource, Limahon opened a canal to the river, and, in the night, escaped with all his people in the small vessels he had constructed. To deceive the Spaniards, and conquer the difficulties opposed to him in the mouth of the river, he set fire to a few small vessels filled with combustibles, and, ordering a false attack to be made on the guard, he, in the meantime, escaped; and, without any obstruction, on the 3d of August 1575, prosecuted his voyage. During these transactions between Juan de Salcedo and Limahon, the Augustine friars held a chapter, and appointed priests in the towns of Candaba and Macabebe, in the province of Pampanga, in Bizan, in the province of Ylocos, and in the island of Negros. They were not satisfied with the innumerable converts, they made in these islands, but they became desirous of attempting the spiritual conquest of the empire of China. There was at that time in Manila, a Chinese of the name of Aumon, who had been sent by the viceroy of Fouquien, in search of Limahon, to promise him pardon, on the part of the Emperor of China, if he would cease his depredations. This Chinese had been to Pangasinan, and told Juan de Salcedo, that he wished to see the pirate; but as Salcedo distrusted the nature of his mission, Aumon deemed it prudent to return to Manila, where he paid his court so well to the Governor, that he delivered him up fifty captives which had been taken from Limahon. Aumon was now desirous of returning to China, and the Augustine friars conceived this would be a good opportunity, to attempt an establishment there. With this view they endeavoured to persuade him, to take two friars under his protection, which request the Governor seconded; and, as the news of Salcedo's success against Limahon had, by this time, reached them, Aumon determined to comply with the request. The friars Martin de Rada, and Geronimo Marin, were nominated for this undertaking, and, at the same time, as ambassadors from the Governor, were the bearers of a letter to the Viceroy of Fouquien, and another to the Emperor, which they were ordered to deliver to the Viceroy, as their directions were not to proceed beyond that point. But as it was intended, that these religious should remain in the province of Fouquien, to propagate the Christian faith, two Spaniards were sent to bring back the answer to the embassy. They left Manila on the 2d of July 1575, and before they returned, the new Governor of these islands arrived.

CHAPTER VIII.

ANNO DOM. 1575.

Of the Administration of Don Francisco La Sande, second Governor of Manila.

DOCTOR Don Francisco La Sande, born at Caceres in Estremadura, and Oidor of Mexico, took possession of this government on the 24th of August 1575. He instituted an inquiry into the conduct of his predecessor, and acquitted him of any misapplication of his authority. At the commencement of La Sande's government, the embassy returned from China, and proved to have had a favourable issue, as the Viceroy of Fouquien received them with great respect; and although he could not permit the friars to remain in the province, as he had no orders to that effect, he forwarded the letter, which the Governor of Manila had written to the Emperor of China, contributing all in his power to second his views: and this fully appeared by the answer, which the Chinese brought in the month of February, the year following, by which the Emperor appointed one port in his dominions, for commercial intercourse with the Spaniards. The Chinese brought considerable presents, which they would not deliver to the actual Governor, but to Guido de Labexares, who, as Governor *ad interim*, had despatched the embassy. This affront Don Francisco La Sande felt so severely, that he behaved to them with great coolness, and made them no presents when they returned. The unhandsome conduct of the Governor, frustrated those expectations, which had been raised by the defeat of Limahon, and the subsequent mission; by making a most unfavourable impression on the minds of the Chinese, who discharged their whole vengeance, on the heads of the two Augustine friars. They landed them in the province of Zambales, scourged them most cruelly, murdered, before their eyes, their interpreter and slaves, and left them bound fast to trees; in which situation they must have perished, had not, providentially, Morones been passing that way, who released them, and cured their wounds.

This year, 1576, was unpropitious to the Spaniards in the Philippines; for, independent of this disgrace, they had the misfortune to lose Juan de Salcedo, who died on the 11th of March, and who had been a second Pizarro, or Cortes, in this conquest. He was seized with a fever while in Ylocos, and when in that state, visiting a mine in his domains, he drank some cold water, which operated so powerfully on the intestines, that he died in three hours. On the island of Catanduanes, likewise, a party of Augustine missionaries was shipwrecked: this was a public loss, and most severely felt, as, without the labours of the religious, the military exploits of the Spaniards, would have been of little avail, in securing the subjection of these islands.

This loss was repaired the following year, by the arrival of some more friars, and seventeen Franciscans, whom the Augustines received in their convents, and assigning to them the ecclesiastical authority over a number of towns, the Franciscans began their labours with indefatigable zeal.

About this time, Queen Elizabeth of England, sent the famous Drake with a considerable squadron, for the purpose of subduing the Moluccas. In passing the Straits of Magellan, he lost several of his ships; but he pursued his course in his own ship, committing many acts of hostility on the voyage, and giving a name to several islands which he discovered, such as St. Bartholomew, St. James, and New

Albion, a large island, where he was detained six weeks. Arriving at Tidore, he began to gather cloves, without permission from the King of the island, at which the latter took great offence; but Drake having made him presents, he stipulated for the assistance of their arms, in case he should require it, permitting the English to establish factories for collecting cloves and nutmegs, and, in token of his amity, sent a most superb ring to the Queen of England. Richly laden with spices and Chinese merchandize, which he had captured in several of our vessels, on their voyage to New Spain, Drake proceeded on his return to England, where, after a variety of disasters, he arrived, filling all Europe with admiration of the valuable nature of his cargo. That strangers might not, by such means, acquire a footing in the Moluccas and neighbouring islands, the Governor sent an expedition against the island of Borneo, which, by the following circumstances, became a matter of easy conquest. Sirela, King of Borneo, had come to Manila, to solicit the assistance of the Spaniards, in the recovery of his kingdom, of which he had been unjustly deprived by his brother; and he promised, in the event of his success, that the whole of this large island, should become tributary to Spain. Don Francisco La Sande, conceiving this a most desirable object, and that it would necessarily lead to the conquest of all the Archipelago of Maluco, determined to go in person, that he might not lose the favourable opportunity, which now presented itself, by replacing Sirela in the possession of his kingdom.

He sailed from Manila in thirty vessels, with a large body of Spaniards and friendly Indians, and arrived safely at Borneo. Having entered the river, he proceeded along it, until he arrived at the residence of the usurper, upon which he immediately directed his artillery. The King, however, with his troops, gallantly attacked the Spaniards, but in a short time, fled in great disorder, and took refuge in the mountains. The Governor placed his deposed brother on the throne, and returned to Manila, where he planned several other expeditions. He sent a squadron to Jolo and Mindanao, which reduced these two islands, and compelled them to pay the customary tribute to the King of Spain; but from the great distance they were at from Manila, and the very limited number of clergy then in the seat of government, a sufficiency could not be spared, for the purpose of converting the natives to Christianity, during the short time these islands were held. He completed the conquest of the province of Camarines by means of Captain Chaves, who founded the city of Nueva Caceres, close to the town of Naga. The Augustine friars began their spiritual conquest, but finding their number unequal to the task, of duly attending the undertaking, they called in to their assistance the Franciscans, to whom eventually they ceded this district.

Towards the close of La Lande's government, an unpleasant disagreement arose between the clergy and laity. The factors had introduced into their respective districts, several abuses, which the clergy would not countenance. Certain services were required of the Indians, beyond the stipulated rents, which were extremely vexatious, and which little accorded with the Christian character. The friars began by preaching against these abuses, but this had little effect, and in the end, so many complaints were made, that it reached the ears of the King (Philip the Second), who issued an order, in which he reproved the conduct of the factors, and enjoined them, to pay strict obedience to the instructions they had received, to confine their imposts to the stipulated rents alone. The Governor gave every aid to the order of his Majesty, making regulations, by which the Indians might be secured against such encroachments in future. This, in some respect, abated the gathering storm, but tranquillity was never completely restored, as the avarice of the factors set at defiance all laws, human and divine.

CHAPTER IX.

ANNO DOM. 1580.

The Administration of Don Ronquillo de Penalosa, third Governor of Manila.

IN April 1580, Don Gonzalo Ronquillo de Penalosa arrived at the port of Cavite, as Governor of Manila. He was a nephew of the famous Judge Ronquillo, who hanged the Bishop of Zamora. He brought to his predecessor, the appointment of Oidor of Mexico, with orders for him to sail by the first ship, destined for Acapulco. On his taking possession of his government, his first step was, to mark out the Chinese quarter of the town, under the guns of the fort of Santiago, on the other side of the river. He sent Captain Rivera to Borneo, again to re-establish on his throne the legitimate King Sirela, who had a second time been deprived of it by his brother, with the assistance of a Portuguese Captain, of the name of Brito. Rivera executed his commission without delay, and returned to Manila, after having placed Sirela in peaceable possession of his kingdom. This was judged to be the fittest opportunity, for bringing the Moluccas under the Spanish dominion, and the Governor began to make preparations for the enterprize, for, in addition to the customary enmity between the courts of Portugal and Castile, he had received positive instructions from Philip the Second, to effect this object. Circumstances, however, compelled him to postpone it till the year following, as several matters of consequence, in these islands, required his presence, particularly in the province of Cagayan, where a Japanese pirate had established himself, with a great many followers and vessels. Pablo Carrion dislodged the Japanese, but not without great loss on the side of the

Spaniards, as the former, rather than be taken prisoners, preferred dying bravely, with arms in their hands. The pirate thus dislodged, the Governor founded the city of Nueva Segovia, close to the Indian town of Lalo, and the city of Arivalo, in the island of Panay, in memory of his native province.

The year following, 1582, an expedition sailed to the Moluccas, commanded by Don Sebastian Ronquillo, a nephew of the Governor, who took with him Pablo de Lima, married to a niece of the King of Tidore, and who, in her right, laid claim to several towns, of which she had been unjustly deprived by the King of Ternate. De Lima was likewise appointed Governor of Ternate, when it should be subdued by the Spaniards, and all these considerations contributed, to induce him to give every aid to this expedition. The squadron arrived at the island of Motiel, and making an easy conquest of it, the natives recognized Pablo de Lima as their chief. From this island, the Spaniards proceeded on their voyage to Ternate, where the Indians seemed determined, to throw every impediment in the way of their disembarkation; but the resistance was of short duration, as the Spaniards contrived to draw them into the interior, and to plant their artillery against the town, without which expedient nothing could have been done. They laid regular siege to the town, and were on the point of taking it, when a disorder in the intestines began to rage among them, which occasioned such mortality, that they were compelled to break up their enterprize, and return to the Philippines. During these transactions in Ternate, the Christians in Manila, found out new objects for mutual hostility. Besides the provinces which I have mentioned, which the Augustine friars had been the means of reducing to obedience, they had distributed priests in Pangasinan, in Cagayan, and in the two provinces of Misames and Caraga, in the island of Mindanao, which are the only two in this large island, acknowledging subjection to the Spaniards. The factor of Mindanao, whose name was Blas de la Serna, treated the Indians with great severity, and lived a scandalous life, highly prejudicial to the cause of Christianity.

The friar whom the Augustines had placed there, admonished him repeatedly to alter his course of life; but as his conduct became more reprehensible every day, the friar, unable to bear it longer, was under the necessity of excommunicating him. The factor, in revenge for (as he termed it) his impudence, publicly beat him. At this time the Bishop of Manila was Don Fr. Domingo de Salazar, who had arrived at Manila in March, 1581, with two Jesuits, who were the first of the order in these islands. On the 21st of December, he erected the church into a cathedral, appointing proper prebends and dignitaries, and forming municipal authorities for its due government. This nobleman was highly attentive to the rights of the clergy. He took up the affair with the factor very warmly, and did not relax in his exertions, until he saw him at Manila undergo the punishment, imposed on him by the sentence of the church, and which he had so well merited.

The whole body of factors being alarmed, and fearing this would be much to their prejudice, persuaded the Governor, to withdraw from the clergy, the Indians who had been given to them for their own service, and that of the church. The Spaniards well inclined to the factors, seconded this advice, and they, in conjunction, commenced a cruel persecution against the Augustine and Franciscan friars. But Pedro de Chaves, Amador de Arriaran, Juan de Morenos, Antonio Savedra, Miguel de Lorca, Francisco de la Cueba, Esteban

Rodrigueze de Figueroa, and other factors, who had seen, of how much importance the friars were, in the conquest and retention of these islands, came over to their party, and defended them against the attack thus made on them, proving satisfactorily, that without the assistance of the clergy, the factors would never have received even their rents.

The Governor, Don Gonzalo Ronquillo, was deeply afflicted at those disputes, so much at variance with his character, and with the anxiety of his views, for the happiness and prosperity of these islands. His whole mind, indeed, was occupied in the consideration, of what might contribute to these ends, and to the aggrandizement of the Spanish name; but unhappily persuading himself, that his honour was committed by these dissensions, he became affected by a deep melancholy, to which he was a prey during six months, and to which he fell a sacrifice in the month of March, 1583, before he completed his third year as Governor. He was interred in the church of St. Augustine, and to do him honour, more tapers than usual being burnt, the roof of the church was set on fire, which in a few hours communicated so generally, that the greater part of the city was destroyed, with immense loss of lives and property.

By the death of Don Gonzalo, his kinsman, Don Diego Ronquillo, succeeded as Governor *ad interim*, being nominated as such in the royal order. The new Governor directed all his attention, to the rebuilding of the city, assisting personally in the public works, and paying particular attention, to the restoration of the houses, belonging to the inhabitants. Such diligence was used, that in a short time, the city was completely re-established. Many of the inhabitants, lost almost all their property in this fire; and the disaster, though of sufficient magnitude, was swelled into a most dreadful picture, by the ship going to Acapulco, but which had been forced by stress of weather into China. It is inconceivable, in what consternation, the inhabitants of the islands in the neighbourhood of Manila, arrived to their assistance. Don Diego Ronquillo immediately sent to China the factor of the royal works, Juan Butista Roman, with orders to chastise those, who had been the cause of spreading this report, and to despatch, at any expense, a ship to New Spain, with a true statement of the extent of the mischief. The factor performed his commission with such efficacy, that the ship he despatched, returned the year following from Acapulco, in company with another; and in these ships came the new Governor and the Royal Audience. The government of Don Diego had lasted only one year, but, though short, it was of great importance to the settlement.

He reduced to obedience in the island

of Layte, and the province of Pangasinan, some towns which refused to pay the usual tribute, and he effectually suppressed symptoms of sedition in the other provinces, and which took their rise in the ill treatment of the factors. The factors entertained the idea, that the Indians whom they had found on their lands, ought to be considered in the light of slaves in every respect, and compelled them to work, appropriating all the wages of their labour to their own use, by which means they enjoyed all the luxuries of life, and even accumulated fortunes. To such a height had these abuses been raised, that a reform was absolutely necessary. The Governor bestowed particular attention on this subject, punishing those who were culpable, and watching over the general good. The result of this was, that many Indians who before had fled to the mountains, returned to the towns, and paid the tribute settled by the government, either in silver, or in the produce of the land they cultivated. By these desirable arrangements, the royal revenue was improved, and the interest of the factors so much injured by their own avarice, that from hence arose the proverb, "Avarice bursts the sack."

CHAPTER X.

ANNO DOM. 1584.

The Administration of Don Santiago de Vera, fourth Governor of Manila.

The Governor, Don Gonzalo Ronquillo, had sent to Madrid Captain Gabriel Rivera, to solicit several objects, necessary to the general welfare of these islands, and in particular, that a Royal Audience should be established there, as it was extremely disadvantageous and embarrassing, to be obliged to have recourse to that of Mexico.

The King granted this request, and sent Don Santiago de Vera, of Alcala de Henares, as Governor and President of the Royal Audience; and Don Melchor de Avalos, and Don Pedro de Roxas, as oidores of it. The third oidor, Don Antonio Rivera, arrived two years afterwards. Don Gaspar de Ayala was nominated fiscal. Don Santiago took possession of his government May, 1584, and immediately formed the Royal Audience, bearing the royal signet with much ostentation, under a canopy, from the convent of St. Augustine, to the palace. The Chancellor was Gabriel de Rivera, who arrived this year, with the title of Mariscal of the lake of Bombon. Immediately that Don Santiago took possession of his government, he put in force the orders which he had received from the King, to chastise those factors, who had abused the authority, they derived from the possession of the lands granted them. He began, by dispossessing Bartoleme de Ledesma, factor of Abuyo, and others the most culpable, punishing the rest in proportion to their irregularities, after full conviction of their delinquency.

In the following year, 1585, he sent Juan de Morones and Pablo de Lima, with a powerful squadron, to reduce the Moluccas under the Spanish dominion, but it returned to Manila with similar disgrace to the preceding one, without being able to take possession of the fortifications of Ternate. The Governor was much chagrined at the ill success of this expedition, and was desirous of repeating the attempt, conformable to the positive instructions received from the King to that effect; but he was not able to execute it, as the troops from New Spain had not arrived, and, independent of this, the insurrections of the Indians were of too formidable a nature, for they lost no opportunity which presented itself of breaking the yoke of the Spaniards. Those of Pampangos and Manila entered into a conspiracy with the Moors of Borneo, who had ostensibly come there for the purpose of traffic. They formed the plan of traitorously entering the town in the night, setting fire to it, and killing in the confusion all the Spaniards.

This conspiracy was discovered by a female Indian, married to a Spanish soldier. The Governor checked it in its commencement, imprisoning many, and severely punishing others by way of example. The islands of Samar, Ybabao, and Leyte, were likewise far from being in a state of tranquillity, and the factor of Dagami, a town of Leyte, had nearly lost his life by the Indians, in the collection of the tribute paid in wax, and which he had attempted to levy by a measure, containing double the usual quantity. This compelled him to fly for safety to the mountains, and he passed from thence in a boat to the island of Zebu. The Governor sent Captain Lorenzo de la Mota to quell these disturbances, which he soon did by promising to punish the delinquent.

Among the calamities which happened during this government, the loss of the ship Santa Anna was not the least; she was on her way, richly laden, to Acapulco, and was taken by the English. Cavendish, an English pirate, emulous of the fame of Drake, having equipped five ships, with the assistance of Queen Elizabeth, took his departure for this quarter of the world; and having committed many acts of hostility on the coasts of Brazil and Peru, he arrived at Molucca, where he procured every information respecting the produce of the Philippines, and the rich cargoes which every year were sent from these islands to Acapulco. Well instructed, likewise, in the tract observed by our galleons, he sailed for the coast of California, to lie in wait for the annual ship destined for New Spain. In due time the Santa Anna, as is customary, made her appearance on that coast, in prosecution of her voyage to Acapulco, and fell into the hands of the English without any resistance, being quite unprepared.

The English having made themselves masters of this valuable prize, directed their course to the Philippines, and arriving at the island of Panay, where we had a ship in the dock of Yloylo, an attempt was made to burn her, but it was rendered ineffectual by Captain Lorenzo de Limas, who made a vigorous resistance, with such soldiers and Indians, as he was able to collect in the province. Abandoning this object, the English commander sent a letter to the Governor, to apprize him of the capture he had made of the Santa Anna, and to inform him he should return frequently to those seas. He departed from Panay for the Cape of Good Hope, from whence he sailed for England, and arrived laden with such riches, that his name became more renowned than ever was that of Francis Drake.

In the year 1589 no ship was despatched to New Spain; for two which had been equipped for this voyage, were lost in the port of Cavite in a dreadful storm, which happened on St. Peter's Day. About the same time many insurrections of the Indians took place, and in particular, those of Cagayan, who were always very troublesome, murdered many Spaniards. Those likewise, in the valley of Dingras, in the province of Ylocos, resisted the collections of tribute, and murdered six people from the city of Fernandina, who were travelling through their towns. Don Santiago quelled these tumults, and restored tranquillity, by duly mingling punishment with clemency. He likewise constructed a strong fort of stone, where the royal gate now stands; he removed to Manila the foundery which was hitherto in Santa Anna; and cast some artillery, with the assistance of an Indian of Pampango. He founded an hospital for the Spaniards: but the principal mover of this pious act was Don Luis de Vivanco, who, jointly with his wife, endowed it, and appropriated it to the reception and cure of the sick. The Governor divided several portions of land among those soldiers and sailors who deserved it most, and conducted himself in the exercise of his authority, so much to the general satisfaction, that his character as an excellent Governor was established by the declaration of the licentiate Herber del Corral, who was chief judge on the occasion of passing his trial of approbation.

CHAPTER XI.

ANNO DOM. 1590.

The Administration of Gomez Perez Dasmariñas, the fifth Governor of Manila.

The clergy of Manila about this period, sent to the court of Madrid and Rome the Friar Sanches, a Jesuit, under the pretence of soliciting some objects, for the spiritual as well as temporal welfare of these islands. Arriving at Madrid, he petitioned that the Royal Audience should be removed, and that Gomez Perez Dasmariñas, a noble Galician knight of the order of Santiago, Corregidor of Logrono, should be sent as Governor. This nobleman arrived at Manila in May 1590, in one of the two ships which the Viceroy of Mexico had despatched, and in which he had sent four hundred troops, a supply, by this time highly requisite in the islands. The other ship which accompanied her struck on a shoal, close in with the land of Maranduque, and was lost, but all the people were saved. The King gave the new Governor, as a salary, ten thousand Castile ducats out of the royal revenue of New Spain, and which was remitted annually to the Philippines.

He brought an order that the proceedings of the Royal Audience should be suspended; and in performance of this, the year following, the Oidores composing it embarked for Mexico; the Oidor Roxas alone remaining, as the *ad interim* successor of the Governor. The Bishop, who had some disagreement with the Governor, feeling the importance of the Royal Audience, as the only tribunal capable of curbing the power of the Governor, and persuading himself it was not safe, to trust in the hands of one man, the uncontrolled exercise of authority, in a country so remote from the seat of government, it was his intention to proceed to New Spain, with a view to procure the re-establishment of the Royal Audience in Manila, and on various affairs of his bishopric. The Governor, that he might not effect his purpose, would not allow him to embark with the Oidores; and the Bishop in the mean time contented himself, with giving full powers and instructions to the Augustine Friar Ortiga, who was going to Madrid, to appear to any allegations which might be preferred against him. In the short time this government lasted, great undertakings were performed; such as building a wall of stone round Manila, erecting the fort of Santiago, and furnishing it with good artillery. The royal magazines in Manila and Cavite were built; and the asylum of Santa Potenciana was erected for the maintenance, at the cost of the state, of a certain number of young persons, daughters of deceased military officers, until they should be married. The Governor established among the different religious orders, a salutary ecclesiastical control over the Indians, assigning to each order their different towns and provinces, and converting the colony into a complete republic; supplying every defect in the government; and putting the whole in a respectable state of defence, by means of his four hundred regular soldiers, divided into detachments.

Among the natives of many adjacent islands which traded with Manila, those of Japan, in particular, brought the richest merchandize for the consumption of the colony, and for the commerce with Acapulco. A keen and able man of this nation, named Faranda Kicmon, who had renegaded from the faith, persuaded Taycosama, Emperor of Japan, to send an embassy to Manila; and promised him, that if he would give him the commission, he would procure him to be acknowledged

King of Manila, and that a regular and lucrative commerce, might be established between the two nations. The Emperor gave credit to his representations, and despatched him with letters to the Governor, claiming the vassalage of the Philippines. The Governor received this embassy, and replied to it immediately, without bringing into question the point of vassalage, by proposing to establish a commercial intercourse; sending for this purpose, the Franciscan Friars Pedro Bautista, Francisco de San Miguel, Bartholome, and Gerardo de San Miguel, who likewise had determined to avail themselves of this opportunity, to establish themselves in that kingdom to preach the gospel: he likewise sent with them a Portuguese of the name of Carvallo, and they bore a handsome present to the Emperor. Notwithstanding many malicious falsehoods which Faranda had circulated, Taycosama received the friars with much courtesy, and granted them permission to remain in his kingdom, treating them with much respect in the first instance, although, at a subsequent period, he murdered them. About this time ambassadors from the King of Camboa arrived, with two elephants, as a present to the Governor; and endeavoured to engage him, to grant them assistance against the King of Siam, who had commenced hostilities against them. The Governor answered the King of Camboa with another present, giving them great hopes, but evading immediate assistance, on the plea that his projected expedition to the Moluccas, required all his resources, however desirous he was of giving the aid they demanded.

That this expedition might not turn out as the former had done, Gomez Perez Dasmariñas determined to accompany it in person. He sailed from Cavite on the 19th of October 1593, and arriving off Santiago, encountered a strong gale from the eastward, and the whole of the fleet was separated, his own ship alone remaining: this compelled him to anchor at Brimstone Cape, to effect which he was obliged to have recourse to his boats, on account of the great variety of currents. The Chinese, to the number of one hundred and fifty, though able to pull at the oar, assisted but very little; and the Governor abused them for the little exertion they made. These people resented this ill-treatment; and considering themselves as superior in force to the few Spaniards in the ship, conceived the design of murdering them the same evening. Whilst the Spaniards took their siesta (or afternoon nap), little dreaming of the designs of the Chinese, the latter commenced their carnage by killing the Governor, and all those who were not able to effect their escape in the launch, or by swimming, sparing only Friar Montilla, a Franciscan, and Juan de Cuellar, secretary to the Governor, whom they took with them. After this massacre they sailed for China, and passing by Ylocos, they entered the port of Sinay to water, where the Indians fell on them, and killed twenty of their number. The following day they disembarked in another port; and actuated by superstitious motives, sacrificed one of the native converts, in revenge for the slaughter the Indians had made the day before, and by which sacrifice, they expected to propitiate their gods in favour of their voyage. They tied him to a cross, and opening his chest, took out his heart, which they offered to their idols. They then made sail, and coasted for several days: they resolved to set on shore Friar Montilla, Secretary Cuellar, and those Philippine Indians who had been their shipmates. They then proceeded to Cochin China, where, in the end, they received the punishment due to their crimes.

On the death of the Governor, the Licentiate Rosas succeeded to the command, and immediately despatched two ships in search of the Chinese, under the command of Don Juan Ronquillo. They made enquiry in several ports; but not being able to gain information respecting their route, they returned without effecting their object. That they might not, however, remain without punishment for such atrocious crimes, and supposing that the Chinese might have taken shelter in the province of Chancheo in China, of which they were natives, he sent Don Fernando de Castro, to solicit of the Viceroy of that province, due satisfaction against the aggressors. Unable, however, to reach that destination, he was, by the interposition of divine Providence, compelled to bear away for Cochin China, where, on his arrival, he found the murderers had retired. He communicated his business to the King, and the whole of them were imprisoned and executed. Some of those, likewise, whom the Portuguese Governor of Molucca, had sent on the expedition with the Chinese, were hanged in Manila. The whole, however, affording small consolation for the melancholy catastrophe which had taken place.

Forty days after the death of the Governor, Friar Montilla and Secretary Cuellar arrived at Manila, after having suffered many severe hardships, and being brought out for death repeatedly, whilst they were with the Chinese. The deceased Governor had given in charge to these gentlemen a trunk, to be delivered to his son Luis Perez Dasmariñas; and on opening it, papers of great importance were found: among the rest, a royal order, by which he had the power to nominate his successor, in virtue of which he named his own son Luis. At first Luis found some difficulty in being acknowledged as such, the Licentiate Roxas being firmly seated, and unwilling to deliver up his authority, for which he had begun to entertain a great attachment; he, however, on the 3d of December, in the same year, left Luis in quiet possession.

The new Governor was desirous of sending another expedition to Molucca, but desisted from it at that time from prudential motives. It was fortunate that he formed this resolution, as in this case, Manila would have been left with only a few troops, and exposed to another attack from the Chinese, on whom little reliance could be placed. Indeed, there was reason to suspect they had something of that nature in contemplation, as many junks about this time arrived with Mandarins in them, and the cause of their appearance was never ascertained. They landed very frequently, and visited the Governor, but did not attempt any thing, nor could he comprehend their object; most fortunately, however, at this moment, arrived the two ships which sailed this year from Acapulco, bringing a sufficient force with them, to resist enemies more powerful than the Chinese.

Our historians have, with great minuteness, stated the losses and arrivals of the ships which are sent to New Spain, on account of their being so interesting to these islands, which depend upon them for their subsistence, and, of course, their loss or arrival occasions a very general sensation. There is no reason to think, that these misfortunes are to be attributed to the difficulty of the passage, nor to stormy weather, so much as to the ignorance of the pilots, who are chosen without examination as to their nautical skill, the bad construction of the ships, their sailing out of season, and too heavily laden. These are, unquestionably, the principal causes of their failure; and it is a pity it is not remedied, for it is with justice affirmed, that the avarice and knavery of some rich people, have buried in the ocean many millions of dollars.

In the year following, the same two vessels again made this voyage, and Señor Morga came in one, as successor to the late Governor, but this nobleman was afterwards promoted to be Oidor of Mexico, where he wrote the history of the Philippines. There came likewise in these ships, a sufficient number of troops, sent by the Viceroy of Mexico. Don Luis Dasmariñas was now, therefore, enabled to give the King of Camboxa that relief which his father had promised. He likewise despatched an expedition to the island of Mindanao; and he quelled an insurrection in some of the provincial towns which had revolted, and refused to pay the tribute, particularly those in Cagayan and Zambales. He did many praiseworthy actions, and governed with more approbation than his father, possessing greater abilities, at

o 2

the same time that he was more affable to all.

In the month of February 1596, the flag ship of the squadron of Alvaro Mendana de Neyra arrived at Cavite. He had sailed from Callao, the port of Lima, with four ships, to colonize the islands of Salmon; and having begun his new settlement in the island of Negros, near New Guinea, he died there, and his wife, Doña Isabela Barreto, at the instigation of the people, left the colony, and came in his ship to Manila. The Governor received her with great attention, and gave her every assistance, to enable her to return to New Spain.

An important establishment was now founded here, called the Pious Work of Mercy, which originated with a clergyman of the name of Losa, and who, together with Captain Esquerra, an inhabitant of Manila, employed themselves in collecting donations for this purpose; and their exertions were so successful, that they were soon enabled to build the college of Santa Isabel, where many female orphans are maintained, and on whom marriage portions are bestowed. In emulation of this pious work, many others were endowed in the convents, and in the cathedral. The projectors traded with their funds to China, Batavia, the coast of Coromandel, and Acapulco, the produce of which was destined to be employed in like manner as above, in hospitals, dowers to orphan females, in ransoming children in China[20], and for masses for souls in purgatory, reserving part of it for the annual increase of the funds of these pious establishments, and to alleviate the distresses occasioned by the losses of the annual ships, of which they thus became the assurers to a certain extent. Such establishments may be useful to new settlers, since the parties desirous of commercial pursuits, may, if they possess any credit, be certain of meeting in these resources a capital with which they may trade. I am not of opinion, however, that they are very useful to these islands, generally speaking, because the rich merchants, who have sufficient capital, employ it in objects attended with no risk, and in their store-houses, and trade with that which they draw from this charity, by which they escape the chance of loss. If there had not, unfortunately we may say, been this resource, no doubt some mode would have been resorted to, of insuring the Acapulco adventures, at less than the pious foundations have been in the habit of contributing, and which often exceeds fifty per cent., and never falls below twenty per cent. Like all other adventures managed by a public body, there is never such strict œconomy as when under the control of individuals, whose interests are involved in the result.

CHAPTER XII.

ANNO DOM. 1596.

The Administration of Don Francisco Tello de Gusman, the fourth Governor of Manila.

THE news of the death of Dasmariñas, reached Madrid through the medium of India, and immediately the King sent as his successor Don Francisco Tello de Gusman, Knight of the order of Santiago, born at Seville, who had been treasurer of the Indies. He arrived at Manila the 1st of June 1596, and the following month despatched the ship San Philip to Acapulco; but she encountered in her voyage heavy gales, was dismasted, and lost her rudder, and having no other resource, bore away for Japan, where the relief she sought was denied, except on the condition of her entering the port of Urando; in effecting which she touched on a sand bank, and made so much water, that she was under the necessity of being unloaded. The Governor, allured by the prospect of such rich booty, immediately conceived the design of making himself master of the vessel and cargo, and accordingly secured it in the royal store-houses, sending information to the Emperor Taycosama, that the Captain having given a false representation of the matter, he had proceeded against him according to law, and had secured the whole of the property. By this means he so warped the whole affair, that the cargo was condemned, and a prosecution was commenced, in the progress of which those Franciscan friars fell martyrs, who had come to this kingdom in quality of ambassadors.

Taycosama named one of the four principal Governors of his kingdom, called Uximonoxo, to take charge of the ship, in order that the cargo might be delivered up; for our Captain, Don Mathias Landecho, had petitioned the Emperor, sending two Spaniards and two friars, of those he had in the ship, with a present worth twenty thousand dollars, to soften him, and, if possible, to obtain justice. Upon their arrival at Meaco, the court of the Emperor, they applied to the Franciscan friars, who, by their experience in this city, they conceived, could procure a favourable reception to their application. The Franciscans judged it better to apply to Ximonoxo, another of the four Governors; but this crafty Japanese, possessing more abilities than the friars, deceived the whole of them, found means to make them deliver up the present of the Emperor to him, offering to give them a letter to Uximonoxo, which they agreed to, and acceded to his wish. The Spaniards returned quite content with this letter; but it was the letter of Uriah, the Hittite, for immediately they delivered it, Uximonoxo imprisoned them. When they found out the deceit, they sent the Friar Guivara to Meaco, to procure their liberty from the other Governors, and, with the assistance of the Franciscan friars, attempted to get an audience of the Emperor, to explain to him the conduct of his Governors; but Uximonoxo was too crafty for them, prejudicing the Emperor against the friars, through the medium of the Bonzos, who are priests of their idols, to whom he suggested the propriety of complaining against them, because they propagated a new doctrine against the gods, which must be prejudicial to the state.

Taycosama, who began to be desirous of keeping possession of the merchandize of the wrecked vessel, imprisoned the Franciscan friars, on pretence of their having preached the gospel of Christ against his command; and likewise pretended that they were employed as spies by the Spaniards, and that, with these views, they had quitted their own country. He now openly seized the property saved, and condemned the friars to death. With them the following were comprehended in this sentence; the Friars Pedro Bautista, Francisco Blanco, Gonsalo Garçia, Francisco de San Miguel, Martin de la Asumpcion, together with Phelipe de Jesus, who was going in that ship to New Spain to be ordained, and had resided with his brethren since his arrival in Japan. These six Franciscan friars, with three Japanese Jesuits, and seventeen Japanese laymen, who professed Christianity, all shared the same fate. They were paraded through the streets of Meaco, with their left ears cut off, and then marched above two hundred leagues into Nangasaqui, where they suffered martyrdom, by being placed on crosses, and put to death with lances. This transaction took place on the 5th of February 1597, in the presence of Señor Martinez, a Jesuit Bishop, many other Jesuits and Franciscan friars, and the Spaniards lately arrived in that ship, and who returned to Manila, after suffering many hardships, and certified what they had witnessed on this occasion.

Immediately on the death of these martyrs being made known in Manila, the Governor sent two Spaniards and an Augustine friar, to solicit their bodies, and complain to the Emperor of the ill treatment which the Spaniards had experienced in regard to their ship, contrary to the treaty which had been made with the government of Manila. They likewise had instructions, to procure the establishment of commercial regulations for the future; and to pave the way for these views, they took with them a present of an elephant, an animal seldom seen in Japan. Taycosama was delighted with this present, and he esteemed it the more, as it knelt three times in his presence, on a certain signal being made to it. He received the ambassadors with great cordiality, and pleaded the laws of the empire, in justification of the conduct which had been observed, with regard to the ship and cargo; but made a promise, for the second time, of protection to the commerce of the Spaniards, assuring them that these vexations should never be repeated, and despatched them with a present to the Governor, together with the relicts of the martyred saints. The Spaniards had little confidence in the duration of this good understanding, for Faranda incessantly instigated the Emperor to commence hostilities on Manila, promising to reduce the whole of the islands to his obedience. The four Governors of the kingdom seconded the representations of Faranda, and measures were adopted with the view of carrying them into effect by collecting an armament; but the chief men of the country, who considered Faranda as a despicable character, much retarded this scheme. It was at first understood in Manila, that this armament was directed against the island of Formosa, as the first step towards the conquest of the Philippines. Our Governor took every precaution, and among others, sent an embassy to Canton, as the Chinese were the ancient enemies of the Japanese; and it was their interest to prevent the latter from making this conquest: nothing of this, however, was eventually necessary, as Taycosama died, and peace immediately followed.

While this was passing in Japan, the two expeditions which Luis Dasmariñas had sent to Camboxa and Mindanao were proceeding in their operations; that which went to Camboxa began successfully, but it was afterwards completely ruined by Major Juan Gallinato, and returned to Manila without effecting any thing. Don Luis Dasmariñas having pledged himself for the success of this expedition, armed, at his own cost, two ships and a galiot, and with the approbation of the Governor, left Manila for Camboxa, and in a little time after arrived at China, at the port of Pinae, twelve leagues distant from Canton, where he encountered the Governor of Malacca, took him prisoner, and returned to Manila. His galiot arrived at Cagayan, and proceeded on his voyage to Camboxa, where he found the King re-established on his throne by the Portuguese, Cabos Diego Belloso and Blas Ruiz. The other two Spanish ships also arrived there, and an attempt was made to establish themselves in that kingdom; but although the King seemed to desire it, they were compelled to abandon the project, as it was opposed by his step-mother, and the Malays had already freed themselves from the control of the Portuguese by the murder of Belloso and Ruiz; indeed a few only had escaped, with Captain Juan de Mendoza in his ship.

In Mindanao, Captain Figueroa, who had the charge of this expedition, and who bore, by the King's order, the title of Marquis of what he might conquer, arrived at Buhayen, where the Moors had some fortifications, from whence he retired to the kingdom of Tamoncaca, whose King was in amity with the Spaniards. The Señor Salazar having come out about this time to see the Royal Audience re-established, the ecclesiastical establishment was likewise arranged, the first Archbishop being the Señor himself. He, however, scarcely enjoyed his dignity three months, as, in August in the same year, he died of a dysentery. There had come with him Friar Pedro de Agurto, of the order of St. Augustine, first Bishop of Zebu, and Señor Benevides, of the order of the Dominicans, first Bishop of New Segovia. In the same year the Oidores arrived, who were to form the Royal Audience, the President of it being the Governor. The chief Oidor was Morga, nominated as successor *ad interim* to the Governor. The others were Don Christoval Telles Almanza, Alvaro Zambrano, and Geronimo de Salazar. In eight days after their arrival, the Royal seal being carried with much pomp to the cathedral, and from thence to the palace, the Royal Audience was, by this ceremony, considered as fully established.

In the garrison of Caldera, Juan Pacho had remained as Governor, and being of an active disposition, he attempted to reduce the natives of Jolo, on which island he landed immediately after a storm of rain, and attacking them, was killed, with the greater part of his people. The residue retreated to Caldera; but in consequence of this defeat, the natives of Jolo and of Mindanao, with fifty Caracoas, invaded the islands of Zebu, Negros, and Panay, pillaging and burning the towns, and making many prisoners. In the following year, 1590, they repeated the attack, and the natives retiring to the mountains, refused to quit them again, as the Spaniards were unable to protect them. Those in particular of the island of Panay were most pertinacious, and would not come near the town, as one of their priestesses had asserted, that the Spaniards were in league with the Moors, and had been the cause of these hostilities for years back. It cost the friars a great deal of trouble, to eradicate the effects of the impression, made by this means on the minds of the Indians, but at length they succeeded, and the towns were re-occupied.

To chastise these insults of the Moors, the Governor sent Juan Gallinato, with two hundred Spaniards, to Jolo; but after making an attempt to possess himself of a fort, which the King of Jolo had on a lofty hill, he returned to Manila, without having effected any thing of consequence.

From that time to the present, the Moors have not ceased to infest our colonies. It is incredible what a number of Indians they have made prisoners, what towns they have plundered, what villages they have annihilated, and what ships they have taken. I am inclined to think, that Providence permits this as a punishment on the Spaniards, for delaying the conquest for no less a period than two hundred years [21], notwithstanding the expeditions and fleets, that have almost annually been sent to attempt it. On the first arrival of the Spaniards in those seas, they conquered, in a short time, all the Philippines, excepting the small island of Jolo, part of Mindanao, and a few other very insignificant islands near them, which, to this period, have not submitted. These Moorish Indians are certainly very valiant, and their enmity has been drawn upon us

P 2

by our own conduct; for instead of following the laudable example of the first settlers in these islands, who brought the natives under subjection, principally by the mild interference of the friars, it seems, of late years, to have been the object of the Spaniards, since the great increase of the lucrative commerce of Manila, to acquire, by oppression and force, lands and establishments on these islands, without any view to conciliate the natives. Those, therefore, who have been sent on different occasions to reduce the country, have, instead of attending to the object of their mission, been solicitous only to serve their own purposes, considering that as a primary, which ought to have been a secondary object; and the natives profiting by constant experience in warfare, during which they discovered that the Spaniards were mortal like themselves, have at last become very formidable. There can be no doubt these Indians may be reduced by the same means employed with the others, that is, by sending missionaries amongst them, and a sufficient number of Spanish stations might be established, to command respect. These garrisons ought to be independent of the Governor of Manila, and ought to have a chief, who should reside there, directing his whole attention to the improvement of the settlement, by the extension in the country of the Spanish influence, by temperate measures.

As the matter is now ordered, these appointments are made with no other view than to enrich, by any means, the individuals sent there as Governors. Such, too, is the situation of the Governors of Zamboanga and Marianas; who appropriate to their own use all the revenue sent by his Majesty's Governors for public purposes, and then return to Manila, leaving the colonies as poor and miserable as the first day they were established.

In October 1600, two Dutch pirates

took their station at the entrance of Marivelez, waiting for the ship Saint Thomas, which was expected to return from New Spain about this time. The Governor sent against them the Oydor Morga with two galleons, an English patache which had come from Malacca, a galiot, and other small vessels. On the 12th of December an engagement took place, when Morga took one ship, and the other fled, very much disabled; but he was incapable of pursuing his advantage, for his ship had suffered so much that she foundered, and fifty of the crew were drowned, the rest being saved on the island of Fortune. The ship which he had taken from the Dutch had on board twenty-five men, whom the Governor ordered to be hanged, as a warning to other pirates. During this year, two ships sailed for Acapulco; one was lost on the island of Catanduanes, but all the people were saved; the other took shelter in one of the Marianas, where she was seized by the Indians, who murdered most of the Spaniards, reserving only a few, whom the ship Saint Thomas rescued on her return to New Spain; but the various disasters which had befallen Manila during this government, were far surpassed by a terrible earthquake, in which many houses, and the church of the Jesuits, were destroyed.

CHAPTER XIII.

ANNO DOM. 1602.

The Administration of Don Pedro de Acuña.

In May 1602, four ships from New Spain arrived at Cavite, in one of which came the new Governor, Don Pedro Brabo de Acuña, Knight of the order of San Juan, and who had been Governor of Carthagena. In passing by the Marianas, he had the good fortune to rescue twenty-five Spaniards, who had been shipwrecked in the St. Margarita. Immediately on taking possession of his government, he gave audience to the ambassadors of Dayfusama, Emperor of Japan, who had succeeded to the kingdom, on the death of Taycosama, and requested that the commerce with his kingdom might be continued; and that shipwrights might be sent from Manila to build vessels for him. Without touching on this last subject, the Governor dismissed the Japanese with a magnificent present, which was all lost, as they were shipwrecked on the island of Formosa. With these ambassadors, friars from all the orders in Manila entreated the Governor to be allowed to proceed to Japan, in order to make converts, even at the risk of martyrdom. These good dispositions and intentions the Governor encouraged, and by his assistance, they were able to establish themselves in that kingdom, where in a short time they founded several convents. In 1603, the Augustine friars already possessed one, and the Captain of the ship Espiritu Santo, who put in there in distress, applied to the friars, requesting them to interest themselves with the Emperor, as the Japanese, conformable to their regulations, would not permit the ship to remain. Dayfusama received the application with courtesy, and punished those who had been the cause of it, sending the Spaniards who had accompanied the friars back to Manila, with great honours, giving at the same time strict orders, that all Spanish vessels arriving in future, in his ports, should be treated as friends; the ship, however, in the meantime had made her escape, fearing the same ill success, as had attended a similar application to Taycosama.

A short time after the arrival of Acuña, he made a voyage through the Bisayas (or Islas de Pintados), to inspect the garrisons, and to make preparations for an expedition, which he intended against the Moluccas; and whilst he was employed in building the fort of Yloylo, the Moors took the opportunity offered by his absence, of seizing all the ships they met with, burning the towns, and endeavouring to take possession of Balayan; but the Alcalde Mayor of the province opposed them; and upon receiving assistance from

Manila, pursued them to a desert island, off which he fell in with the Governor on his return to the capital. Orders were issued to attack them; but the Moors making all the sail they could, he was able only to take two, and sink five others, out of seventy vessels, of which their force consisted. On his arrival at Manila, the Governor received the melancholy intelligence of the death of Señor Tello, his deputy, who had discharged his trust with great zeal and probity. He was buried in the church of St. Augustine, to which he had left considerable donations. Soon after this a great fire happened in Manila, which burnt two hundred and fifty houses, the convent of St. Domingo, and the hospital for the reception of the Spaniards.

In May 1603, three Chinese Mandarins arrived, on the extraordinary mission of discovering, whether the port of Cavite was composed of gold, as a Chinese, called Tiongon, had reported to his Emperor, by whom he was imprisoned, until the truth of his assertion should be ascertained, this man having promised to conquer it or lose his life. It was believed that this was a mere stratagem, to reconnoitre the cou try, as it was understood, that the Emperor intended to land an hundred thousand men, in the following December, with the view of becoming master, of the whole of the Spanish possessions. The Governor treated these Mandarins, with the most flattering distinction, shewed them the island of Cavite, and undeceived them in regard to the opinion propagated by their countryman, assuring them that the island was termed the Golden Island, on account of its lucrative commerce only.

The expected armament of the Emperor did not makeits appearance; but an insurrection of the Chinese inhabitants of Manila followed, which had been in a state of preparation during the embassy, and now broke out. There was a Chinese in

Manila of the name of Engcan, who had remained there since the time of Limahon, who had been baptized, was very rich, and was in intimacy with many Spaniards. He offered to his countrymen, to build a wall round their quarter of the town: the work was commenced; but the fidelity of the Chinese beginning to be suspected, the Governor endeavoured to ascertain their intentions, through the medium of their enemies, the Japanese, from which circumstance the Chinese entertained a belief, that the Governor proposed to massacre them, with the assistance of these people; and they resolved, among themselves, to enter Manila on the eve of St. Francis, and murder every Spaniard in the place. Twenty-five thousand Chinese were concerned in this plot, which was discovered by an Indian having given notice of it to the curate of Guiapo, through whose means the information was instantly communicated to the Governor. There were two classes of Chinese at that time in Manila. Those who came annually for the purposes of commerce, and those who had long been residents, in a quarter of the town called Parian, outside of the walls of the city, and whom the Dominican friars had endeavoured to convert.

The first step the Governor took, was to attempt to reconcile the annual Chinese merchants, who were very numerous; but he failed in the attempt, as they had collected in a large body in open rebellion, in a town within half a league of Manila, the others remaining in Parian. The Governor made a confidant of Engcan, and sent him, in company with some Spaniards, to endeavour to bring them back to a sense of their duty, but without effect, as the works they had raised in their defence would, in their opinion, protect them. In the night, some of them sallied out, burned the towns of Quiapo and Tondo, and killed many Indians. They were opposed by an hundred and thirty Spaniards, almost all of whom perished: among them were Don Luis Dasmariñas, Don Thomas Brabo, and Don Juan de Alcega, whose heads the Chinese sent to Parian, as an incitement for their countrymen to follow their example. Upon examination, it being discovered that Engcan was the principal abettor of these men, he was imprisoned, which had such an effect upon many of his countrymen, that they hanged themselves in despair.

The Spaniards, finding that they could do nothing by means of mild measures, commenced their operations, and fought with such determined resolution, that the slaughter was immense. So general was the spirit of loyalty, that even the friars took up arms, and, in particular, Antonio Flores, who had been a soldier in Flanders and Italy, and had, in the battle of Lepanto, been ensign under Bernardino de Meneses, but afterwards took the habit of St. Augustine. The position he took was on the river, close to which the rebels were obliged to pass to join the Chinese of Parian; from this he sallied out, and made great slaughter among them. They made good their retreat, however, to Parian and Dilao, where they threw up works, but Captain Gallinato burned Parian, and laid waste Dilao; and Captain Luis de Velasco pursued them to Tabuco, which we now call Cabuyao. The Chinese not being able to maintain themselves here, passed on to the town of St. Pablo in the mountains, where Velasco, who had pursued them, fell, together with two Franciscan friars. Here the insurgents fortified themselves so strongly, that it was deemed necessary to send a greater force from Manila against them.

Major Christoval de Acuna was charged with the expedition. He cut off their supply of provisions, and reduced them to such distress, that their only alternative was, to abandon their position or starve.

They availed themselves of the cover of night, and made the best of their way to Batangas, where the Spaniards pursued them, and completed their destruction, having killed in different engagements, twenty-three thousand men, one hundred alone, who were rowers in the galleons, remaining of their whole number; and as a warning to their countrymen, to abstain from insurrection in future, Engcan was ordered to be hanged, and his head to be placed on the gaol. The Governor sent two Augustine friars to Spain, to inform his Majesty of the rebellion, and to enable them to arrive in a shorter time, he sent them by India; but they encountered so many difficulties in their passage through Goa, Persia, Turkey, and Italy, that it was three years before they arrived at the court of Madrid. This has always been a dangerous journey, and was particularly so to Friar Nicholas Milo, an Augustine, who, a few years before, had been sent the same route with a lay brother, born in Japan, and who, after having been exposed to great misery in many countries, fell a martyr in Muscovy with his companion. The Emperor of China sent ambassadors to Manila respecting the rebellion, requesting to know the meaning of the slaughter, which had been made among his subjects. The Governor justified himself amply, and the commerce remained on the same footing as before.

In March 1604, eight hundred troops arrived from New Spain, with which relief Don Pedro de Acuña was enabled to fit out a fleet of thirty sail, in the port of Yloylo, for the conquest of the Moluccas. He sailed at the head of this armament on the 15th of January, 1606; and upon his arrival at Ternate, he sat down before the place, to which the King of the island had retired, and took it on the 1st of April, with the loss of fifteen Spaniards. The King of Ternate, who had fled with some of his subjects, intimated a desire to enter into amicable terms with the Spaniards, proposing to deliver up all his fortresses, the towns in Batoquina, which were anciently peopled by Christians (either Dutch captives, or Spanish deserters), all his Christian prisoners, the islands of Marotay and Herrao, with all his artillery and ammunition; and which terms were acceded to. He was not, however, left in possession of his kingdom, but accompanied the Governor to Manila, with some of his chiefs, who were not allowed to remain, from an apprehension of their fomenting disturbances.

The Colonel, Don Martin Esquival, was appointed Governor of Ternate, with six hundred men; and in Tidore, the King of the island requested, that Captain Alarcon might remain with one hundred

Q 2

troops, which was acceded to. During these transactions, and while this armament was at Ternate, and few troops remained at Manila, the Japanese who lived behind the city, availed themselves of these circumstances, and took up arms against the Spaniards. This rebellion was soon put a stop to, through the mediation of the friars, who persuaded the insurgents to lay down their arms, and submit quietly. By this species of management, time was gained for the arrival of the Governor, to whom information had been sent. He arrived at Manila, banished the ringleaders to their own island, and obliged the rest to live in the town of Dilao, where they would be always under our guns; and by this means, kept in obedience. The Governor reaped little benefit from these successes, as he was immediately afterwards, seized with a complaint in the intestines, which carried him off on St. John the Baptist's day. On the death of the Governor, Don Christoval Telles de Almanza, as chief Oidor, became Military Governor *ad interim.* The rebellion, which lay smothered in the breasts of the Japanese, on this occasion, broke out afresh. They engaged the Spaniards, and many fell on both sides, as the Japanese were very brave, and were called the Spaniards of Asia. In the end, however, they were conquered, and were not permitted to live together in any considerable number till the year 1621, when Pelayo Hernandez built shops on their old quarter, which were hired out for the benefit of the Franciscan friars.

Some of the Spaniards of the Moluccas took prisoner Pablo Blancardo, the Dutch commander at Malacca, and brought him in his galley to Ternate. The Governor there, in consideration of fifty thousand dollars, set him and all his people at liberty, which, when it was known in Manila, was stigmatized as an act of great baseness; and this public censure affected the Governor's mind to that degree, that he died of grief soon afterwards. The second in command succeeded; and to give satisfaction to the Royal Audience, despatched two ships in search of General Blancardo, who, it was supposed, had gone towards Maquien, in a patache; they took him prisoner a second time, and sent him with all his people, to Manila, where he was some time afterwards repaid from the Royal coffers, the amount of his ransom. Pablo Blancardo died of grief in prison at Manila, where he had been confined until the arrival of twenty-two Spaniards, who had been taken at Amboyna by the Dutch, and for whom it was intended he should be exchanged.

The Royal Audience conducted themselves with great approbation in the civil administration, until the year 1608, when Don Rodrigo Vivero of Laredo, who was named by the Viceroy as Governor *ad interim*, arrived at Manila, and having had great experience in the management of the Indians in New Spain, he availed himself of it on this occasion, giving instructions to that effect to the chief judges, and other ministers of justice. He governed with much satisfaction for one year, when he delivered up the insignia of his office, and returned to Mexico.

CHAPTER XIV.

ANNO DOM. 1609.

Of the Administration of Don Juan de Silva.

WHEN the account of the death of Acuña reached Madrid from New Spain, the government was bestowed on Don Juan de Silva of Truxillo, Knight of the order of Santiago, who, at that time, was serving in Flanders. He arrived at Cavite in Easter, and took possession of his government, bringing with him six companies of soldiers, which addition to our force was of great importance at this period, as, in the month of October, the Dutch squadron which has been mentioned, appeared off the port of Yloylo. It was composed of six ships and a considerable military force, which it was intended to disembark in this province, but they were repulsed by the Alcalde Mayor. It then appeared off Marivelez, with the view of preventing ships from going to Manila, and of seizing all merchantmen. Don Juan de Silva fitted out an armament, with which, in the month of April, he attacked and defeated them on the day of St. Mark. He took two ships, the Captains of which had been killed, with many of the crews; a third fled, and the other two which had been separated the day before from the fleet, and were returning with great booty, retired with such despatch, that the Spanish squadron was unable to come up with them. He, however, seized those ships which they had taken. Among others was a Japanese vessel, in which were embarked those Spaniards, who had been wrecked on the coast of that island in the ship St. Francis.

The Archbishop of Manila, Benavides,

having died on the 26th of July, 1605, his Majesty named as his successor, Don Diego Vasques Mercado of Arevalo, in Old Castile. This year, 1610, he arrived at the Philippines, and discharged his functions with great approbation, until the year 1616, when he died, and the Bishop of Zebu succeeded him in the Archbishopric.

The Dutch being settled in the island of Java, and possessing fortifications in Malacca and other parts of India, our Governor had little relish for such a neighbourhood, and as they had at times infested our seas, and attacked our islands, he determined, in person, to destroy the forts they had in Malacca, which being so close in his vicinity, he was the more jealous of. He fitted out a squadron of six ships and two galleys, and sailed for Ternate, where he intended to take on board some linguists, and to arrange all his other operations. He understood, in Ternate, that the Dutch hearing of this expedition, had fortified themselves in such a manner in Malacca, that it was impossible to make an impression upon them, and that he might not entirely lose the benefit of the armament he had prepared, he attempted to reduce the forts in Gilolo and Bata-quina, but was obliged to retreat to Manila, with the loss of three hundred men, when he immediately began to make preparations of men and ships for another expedition of the same nature. These islands, at this time, received considerable aid in the arrival from Spain, by the way of India, of five caravelas out of seven, which in April, 1613, had sailed from Cadiz, commanded by Ruy Gonzalez de Segueira, having on board three hundred and fifty soldiers, two hundred and forty seamen, and a hundred Portuguese landsmen.

Upon the arrival of this relief, the Governor determined to proceed to Malacca against the Dutch, whose position he ordered to be reconnoitred, but he found them so powerful in ships, which had arrived by the Straits both of Magellan and Sunda, that he deemed it necessary to use his utmost exertions, to enable him to cope with such powerful enemies. With this view he sent a despatch to the Viceroy of India, requesting he would unite the forces of the two kingdoms; but while he was preparing his armament at Cavite, ten Dutch vessels arrived at Panay. They landed a number of men, and marched for the city of Arivalo, burning the churches and the convents of the Augustine friars, in the towns of Ogtong and Xaro. The Indians, aware of the inadequate force the Spaniards possessed, fled to the mountains, and although the Dutch retired immediately, it cost the friars a great deal of labour, to bring them back to their towns, where they could not persuade themselves they were secure.

By the end of the year 1616, Don Juan

de Silva had collected the greatest armament, that had been seen in the Philippines; it consisted of ten galleons, four galleys, a patache, and many smaller vessels, with all necessary supplies, and five thousand men, two thousand being Spaniards and Portuguese. He sailed with this formidable armament, on the last day of this year, to attack the forts of Malacca; but as the galleons had not arrived which were expected from India, and which he imagined had wintered in the Straits of Malacca, and it was known that the Dutch kept some vessels in these Straits, in expectation of the ships from China which passed by here, the Governor thought it most adviseable, to attack these ships in the first instance, and after he had destroyed them, he should be able to join the galleons from India, and proceed to the Dutch forts in Malacca. The reasoning was good, but it failed in the execution, the galleons of

India having been burnt, in an engagement they had with the Dutch, and the latter having quitted the Straits eight days before the Spaniards arrived, flying with all their effects, as they had received secret intelligence of their route. At the same time that the Spanish galleons entered the Straits, two Malay merchantmen from China arrived very richly laden; by saving which, the inhabitants of Malacca called Don de Silva their preserver, received him on shore under a canopy, and expected from his valour, and the powerful fleet he brought, that India would be freed from those freebooters, the Dutch; but he was seized with a fever, and died in eleven days, on the 19th of April, 1616. He had ordered his body to be embalmed, and directed it should be carried to Xerez de los Cavalleros, to a convent of bare-footed carmelites, and buried there. Before he died, he gave the command of the armament to

Don Alonzo Henriquez, who brought it back to Manila, without effecting any thing else.

By the death of the Governor, the command devolved on Don Andres Alcaraz, the oldest Oidor, who had been left in charge of the government by Don Juan de Silva, when he sailed with the armament for Malacca. About the same time our squadron sailed from the bay, another Dutch squadron, which had lately arrived by the Straits of Magellan, entered the mouth of the harbour, and lay a month close to Marivelez. There were only four ships and two pataches laying before Manila, and it was without artillery, ammunition, or soldiers. The Governor *ad interim* was not dismayed at this; he armed those few ships he possessed, fortified certain positions, and was encouraged in the undertaking by the people, who took up arms, not only the laity, but even the ecclesiastics also. The Dutch commander wrote two letters to the Royal Audience, and one to General Pablo Blancardo, whom the Spaniards had carried prisoner to Manila; but as soon as he learned that Blancardo had died in prison, he made sail to the Moluccas.

Upon the death of Silva, the Dutch came with ten ships against Oton, where they were gallantly repulsed by the commandant of the Pintados, Don Diego de Quiñones, who, in a wooden fort, sustained a siege of ten days, during which time the Dutch made four assaults, in which many were killed, but at last they were compelled to re-embark, and they retired to Malacca. The following year the same armament of ten ships came against Playa Honda. The Governor despatched against them, the Colonel Don Juan Ronquillo, with six galleons and two galleys; they came to an action on the 14th of April, 1617, and the two commodores being engaged, Don Juan Ronquillo sunk his adversary's ship, called the Sun of Holland; two other ships were burnt, and the rest fled with precipitation. The Spaniards, however, were not able to pursue them, as they had suffered much in the engagement, and had lost the galleon St. Mark. After this action, Don Geronimo de Silva returned from Molucca, and the Oidor Alcarez resigned to him his office, the duties of which he had discharged with great applause. In October, Don Geronimo ordered the seven galleons that had been so severely handled in the last engagement, to be laid up in Marinduque. The two ships for Acapulco were despatched in the worst season of the year, during the hurricane months, and they were both lost, one on the coast of Lobo, and the other on that of Galban. This reflected no great credit on the wisdom and prudence of the Governor.

CHAPTER XV.

ANNO DOM. 1618.

The Administration of Don Alonzo Faxardo.

On the 2d of July, 1618, arrived Don Alonzo Faxardo, of the order of Alcantara, of Murcia, and on the day following he took possession of the government of these islands. His Majesty had appointed him chief of an armament which he had intended to send by the Straits of Magellan, to the relief of Don Juan de Silva, to drive the Dutch from these seas; but it was delayed by his sending the forces destined for the Philippines, to the relief of the Emperor of Germany, Ferdinand the Second. The voyage on this account did not take place, until the death of Silva was known, when his Majesty named Faxardo as Governor, charging him to be careful of the interests of the Indians, who had suffered much in the late struggles, and promising ample rewards to those Spaniards, who should make this an object of their special attention.

A short time after his arrival, the Dutch appeared in those seas, not with the intention of attempting Manila, as they were aware of the difficulty of the undertaking, but to intercept the galleons from Acapulco, richly laden with bullion. For this purpose they cruized with three ships off Cape Espiritu Santo, taking their station in the strait of St. Bernardino, as the galleons coming from Acapulco were in the constant habit of taking that route. On the 25th of February the Dutch got sight of them; they bore up, and ordered them to strike their colours, when a severe engagement took place. The Spaniards, under the veil of night, and in the confusion which prevailed, separated and escaped, one arriving at Palapag, and the other at Borongo, on the coast of Ybabao, where the cargoes were all saved, though the ships were lost. That the same misfortune might not occur again, the Governor ever after gave the commanders secret instructions, changing their route each voyage. On the 24th of August, this year, Friar Miguel Garcia Serrano, of the order of St. Augustine, late Bishop of New Segovia, took possession of the Archbishopric of Manila.

In the year 1623, upon the canonization of St. Ignacio and St. Francisco Xavier, the friars of that order celebrated a grand festival, and those of Zebu, desirous of imitating them, likewise celebrated one, at which all the Jesuits of the island of Bohol were present, leaving very few Spaniards in that island. The defenceless state of it induced two or three Indians to persuade the rest to rebel, assuring them that the Devil had appeared, ordering them not to pay tribute to the Spaniards, but to retire to the mountains, and erect a chapel, where they should worship him, and he would give them every thing they required, and defend them from the Spaniards. This was quite sufficient to set all the island in a flame, two towns alone remaining faithful to the Spaniards. The Alcalde Mayor of Zebu, immediately upon notice of this insurrection, sent fifty Spaniards, and one thousand friendly Indians to Bohol, who attacked the rebels with great vigour, made considerable slaughter, and completely routed them. This ought to have undeceived them, but they were obstinate, and fortified themselves on a rock, which, however, afforded them little defence, as our people being protected by their shields from the arrows and stones they hurled down, gained the height, and made great havock among them, making prisoners all that were not able to save themselves by flight. The Alcalde Mayor hanged some of the ringleaders, and pardoned the remainder; but insensible to this favour, they spurned at the proffered pardon, and fled to the mountains, to which, six months after, the Alcalde returned, and thoroughly quelled the insurrection.

The bad example of the people of Bohol was followed by those of the island of Leyte, and was fomented by an Indian who was not suspected of disaffection. This was Bancao, a petty chief of Dimasava, who had received Legaspi with great attention, and had accompanied him to Zebu, where he was baptized, for which conduct Philip the Second had sent him a royal order, granting him many privileges. He had been very faithful to the Spaniards in his youth, but turned traitor in his old age. In imitation of those of Bohol, he raised an insurrection among the Indians in the island of Leyte, so that it became necessary to send a force against them.

Although they saw the Spaniards were superior in numbers to them, they were not dismayed, and received them firmly; but in a short time they fled with precipitation. In this flight Bancao was killed, having been transfixed by a lance: his head was placed on a pole, to serve as a warning to others, which had so good an effect, that order was immediately restored.

This year an expedition was sent to the mountains of Igorrotes, where there were mines of gold, and where the Indians were of fairer complexion, with the small eyes of the Chinese. It was imagined that when Limahon was in Pangasinan, many of his people, pressed by hunger, fled to the mountains, and mixed with the inhabitants, from which intercourse resulted this cast, so different from the rest.

This expedition, under charge of Francisco Carriño de Valdes, head of the provinces of Pangasinan and Ylocos, marched in good order seven days, and on the eighth arrived in the town of the mines, where the natives received them well; but the Spaniards placed too much confidence in them. The Igorrotes, when least expected, rose on them, and treacherously murdered the chief of the friendly Indians, on which de Valades retired, to wait a better opportunity. The following year the expedition was expected to be repeated, but it was not, as it became necessary for the troops to march to Cagayan, to quell an insurrection among the Indians of that province. Many expeditions have since taken place to these mountains, but with such ill success, that the Indians of this district remain independent to this hour. They, however, trade with the Spaniards in gold, wax, and tobacco, in return for cattle; and the Augustine friars have succeeded, in converting to Christianity, a few who live in the towns near the mountains.

The Governor persevered in pacific

measures as much as possible, although those measures were deemed disgraceful. He had much domestic uneasiness on account of his wife, Dona Catalina Zembrano, who had an illicit connection, and was accustomed to steal out from the palace to a particular house, where she was at last discovered with her lover by Faxardo, who going his rounds through the city, as was his custom, from information, no doubt, which he had received, entered into the house in which this lady was with her paramour, and found her in a situation, which rendered her guilt sufficiently manifest. Don Alonzo, a man of high honour, severely felt this injury, and was determined to take proper vengeance. He ordered a confessor to be called to her; and the ceremony at an end, unmoved by the tears and persuasion of the priest to the contrary, he stabbed her with his own hand. The unworthy paramour saved his life by flight, and thus escaped the vengeance of the Governor. Don Alonzo soon after fell into a profound melancholy, of which he died in two years, and was buried in the church of the Franciscans, August, 1624. By his death Don Geronimo de Silva succeeded to the military government, and the civil government became vested in the Royal Audience. In a short time after, a fleet of seven Dutch men of war appeared off Playa Honda, and many of their soldiers landed on the island of Corrigidor, and took prisoners or killed such Indians as fell in their way. The Governor proceeded against them with five galleons and two large galleys, and fell in with them on the coast of Playa Honda, when the Dutch attempted to escape; but our commander's ship, by superiority of sailing, prevented it, when a warm engagement took place, and a Spaniard was killed close to the Governor. It is necessary to mention this accident, as he thought himself in great danger, and was so alarmed by it, that he ordered the ships to retire to Cavite, where he was received with the contempt he merited; the people imputing the loss of the victory to his cowardice. Complaints were made to the Royal Audience, who confined him in the fort of Santiago, where he remained until he was released by the Governor who succeeded him, *ad interim*, Don Fernando de Silva, knight of the order of Santiago.

Don Fernando had been in Manila before this time, having there made a most honourable matrimonial connection; and having accumulated a good fortune, he went with his wife to Mexico, and from thence to Madrid, having been sent thither by his near relation, the Viceroy of New Spain, Marquis de Cerralbo. Having returned to Mexico and this vacancy in the government of Manila occurring, it was given to him *ad interim,* and he arrived there in June 1625.

He was received in Manila with great satisfaction, as they knew he was prudent, and well acquainted with these islands: this he had sufficiently shewn in the measures he had adopted for the protection of our commerce, by means of the ships he had built at Cavite for that purpose. He ordered the Alcalde Mayor of Cagayan to land on the island of Formosa, and fortify it in that part of Fanchuy which was the nearest to Cagayan, in order, with greater facility to oppose the Dutch, who, the year before, had raised forts on the opposite side, called Tayguan, with the intention of obstructing the commerce of China with Manila. The Alcalde Mayor executed his commission, and constructed works sufficiently extensive to accommodate the troops, and the Dominican friars, who had gone there to convert the natives; and who exerted themselves with such zeal, that in a short time they built several towns, and were able to number the greater part of the natives, among the professors of our faith.

CHAPTER XVI.

ANNO DOM. 1626.

Of the Administration of Don Juan Niño de Tabora.

Don Juan Niño de Tabora, knight of the order of Calatrava, was named as Governor of the Philippines. He embarked for his government with six hundred troops, and several officers, who had served with him in Flanders, among whom were Don Lorenzo Olaso y Ochotegui, who came with the appointment of Colonel. Tabora arrived safely at Manila, and entered upon his government on the 29th of June, 1626. He possessed a fund of military knowledge, which was of great importance, at this period, to the Philippines, and he immediately provided a sufficient force to protect their commerce, and secure the respect of their neighbours. In ten months after his arrival, he had collected eight large ships of war, four smaller for the commerce of Acapulco, and two still smaller for the protection of the intercourse with Molucca. With this armament, and with two ships, which were expected from New Spain with men and money, he determined to attack the Dutch on the island of Formosa; but the arrival of the two ships being retarded very considerably, he was not ready to proceed with the expedition, until the middle of August. The Royal Audience, considering the approach of the monsoon, and apprehensive of the loss of the squadron, and that the object of the expedition might be thus defeated, represented their fears to the Governor, and passed an order that it should not sail. Having no faith, however, in what he considered as idle chimeras, Tabora left Cavite, and arrived at Cape Boxeador; where, finding the north winds had set in, and that it was impossible to make head against them, after repeated unsuccessful attempts, he bore away for Cavite; and the only advantage resulting, from his pertinacious opposition to the opinion of the Royal Audience, was the relief he sent in some small vessels, to the Spaniards in the island of Formosa.

A vessel soon after arrived from China, and gave the intelligence that the Dutch were lying in wait at Macao, for the merchantmen expected from Manila in China. The Portuguese requested, that part of the armament might be allowed to convoy them, offering to contribute to the expenses. The Governor, accordingly, sent with them two large galleons, with a patache, ordering the commodore, after he had seen the Portuguese safe, to run up the coast from Macao to Sincapura in search of the Dutch, wintering at Siam, for which indulgence he was ordered to make the necessary presents to the King. Don Juan de Alcaraz, who was the commodore, punctually obeyed his orders: he arrived at Macao, and not meeting with the Dutch, who had quitted it precipitately, on notice of his appearance in this quarter, he passed on to Siam, where, finding the Dutch protected by the Siamese, he burned some of their junks, and made prisoners the ambassadors whom the Siamese were accustomed, at certain periods, to send to China, with their acknowledgment of the sovereignty of the Emperor. Upon this occasion our arms acquired such credit, that, during the whole of this government, the Dutch made no further attempt against these islands.

In the year 1628 two ships arrived with the usual supplies from Acapulco, and in them came Friar Hernando Guerrero, of the order of St. Augustine, Bishop of Cagayan, and the Governor's intended bride, Doña Magdalena Zaldivar y Mendoza, with whom he had entered into a treaty of marriage while at Mexico, and had obtained leave from the King for that purpose. The wedding feasts, however, were no impediment to the operations of the government. The Moors of Jolo continually infested these islands; those, in particular, which were the more remote from the capital, were kept in perpetual alarm, and nothing was talked of but the depredations committed, and the prisoners taken. To chastise these insults, a squadron was sent against Jolo, under the command of Don Christoval de Lugo. He arrived safe, and landed all his people without any resistance, the Indians having, in a cowardly manner, abandoned their town, and retired, with their King, to a fort situated on the top of a hill. The Spaniards plundered these houses, in which the friendly Indians diligently assisted, enriching themselves by the spoils, which consisted of rice, gunpowder, brimstone, small-arms, &c. They did not pursue them to the fort on the top of the hill, in which they had taken refuge; but, after having completely destroyed the town, they embarked for Manila. In passing by the island of Basilan, they landed, burned the principal town, and destroyed all the trees, as a punishment for the aid which these Indians had afforded to those of Jolo, in the last incursions they made.

The following year, a sacrilege was committed in the cathedral, which affected the mind of the Archbishop to that degree, that he died of melancholy. He was one of the most devout prelates who had occupied the archbishopric. He was interred in the church of St. Augustine.

After his death, there was a dispute between the ecclesiastical Cabildo and the Bishop of Zebu, as to who should succeed *ad interim* to the archbishopric, when the Royal Audience determined in favour of the Bishop, conformable to the bull of

S 2

Pius V. The Moors in Jolo and Caumocones again commenced their ravages in the islands: nothing was secure in the towns on the coasts; neither friars, Indians, churches, or ornaments; all were objects of their enmity. Notice was, without loss of time, given to the Governor; he despatched a fleet, commanded by Don Lorenzo Olaso, for the double purpose of making peace with the Indians of Mindanao, as they requested, and to retaliate upon those of Jolo. He arrived at Jolo, landed his people, and marched up to the fort on the hill, to which, as usual, the Indians had retired. The General believed it no difficult matter to reduce the fort, and gave orders to attack it accordingly; he shewed, in the attack, great personal valour, and acting the part of a common soldier, as well as a general, was, with two of his captains, killed. As no officer remained to command them, the men retired to their ships; and, without doing any thing else than laying waste the country, they returned to Manila in haste, and in disgrace, the Moors becoming more insolent than they were before. The Indians of the province of Caraga, in Mindanao, observing that the Spaniards were unable to subdue their countrymen, put to death some of the friars and Spaniards who were living among them, and declared open rebellion in most of the towns of the province.—The remaining friars and Spaniards, took refuge in the towns which continued faithful to their cause; and, in a short time, relief arriving from Manila, order was again restored.

This year several embassies arrived at Manila: one from Japan from the Governor of Nangasaquy; and the King of Saxuma, likewise, sent ambassadors, seeking redress for the ravages our galleons had committed in the harbour of Siam, on two junks of his nation, and out of which had been taken some of the royal merchandize, which they considered a great sacrilege, and which had so irritated them, that the real object of the embassy was to reconnoitre the place, with a view to take vengeance for this insult. A Governor of one of the Chinese provinces, sent an embassy to request the continuation of the commercial intercourse; and the King of Cambodia, who was at war with the King of Siam, sent to request the protection of the Spaniards, offering the commerce of his kingdom, and liberty to form a dock for the building of ships. The Governor received all these with presents, and dismissed them with urbanity and kindness: he accepted the offer of the King of Cambodia, and sent some ship-builders for the purpose of constructing a vessel there: with them went four Dominicans to preach the gospel; but when they arrived, finding the King dead, and little disposition in his son, who succeeded him, to admit the catholic religion, they all returned to Manila without effecting any thing.

The Governor, who was determined to

lose no opportunity that offered to build ships, finished one in the port of Cavite; but so badly constructed, that, at the commencement of her voyage for Acapulco, she foundered in the port: she was, however, hove up, and sufficiently repaired to proceed on her voyage the following year. By this means, and the arrival here of the other ships in 1631, no ship remained in Acapulco to send to the Philippines; and the Viceroy of Mexico despatched two pataches with the ordinary relief. In one of these came Don Francisco Roxas y Oñate, Oidor of Mexico, as inspector of the Royal Audience, and other tribunals; and his office to continue two years. He was well received, and the Governor supported his authority whilst he lived; by means of which, he made his visit pleasant, although he suspended two Oidors. His Excellency, on the 22d of July 1632, died of a dysentery, occasioned by being exposed to the rain and sun, during his visits to and from Cavite, in the performance of his office, in which he was extremely diligent, having made a bridge over the river of Manila, repaired the fortifications of the town, and constructed several works in Cavite.

Don Lorenzo Olaso had been named by the Viceroy of Mexico to succeed him *pro tempore*. Nothing particular occurred under his administration, which only lasted a year, when Don Juan Zerezo of Salamanca was appointed to succeed as Governor *ad interim*. Immediately on his arrival at Manila, with a view to repress the insults of the Moors, and on the representation of the Jesuits, he determined to form a garrison at Zamboanga. He appointed Don Juan de Chaves to the command, with an adequate force, and orders, after destroying the towns of the Moors, to erect a fort in the situation which Friar Vera had pitched upon, a little distant from the port of Caldera, where it was necessary to maintain a detachment to guard the shipping. This situation is most beautiful; but, having no water, the defect was supplied by digging a channel from the river, through which the water flows in great abundance, and, passing by the wall of the fort, falls into the sea. The first stone of the fort was laid on the 23d of June, 1635. Many of the Spaniards opposed this plan under different pretexts, and experience has shewn what little purpose this fort has answered, its only use being to enrich one military man, who is Governor for three years, and who draws twenty or thirty thousand dollars profit from the supplies furnished the soldiers. The Moors, not in the least checked by the fort of Zamboanga, have continued, to this hour, committing the same ravages as before; and the Indians, who are each taxed a measure of rice for its maintenance, have received neither security or benefit from it.

It has been too justly observed by

Señor Solorzano, that whatever is established with a view to benefit the Indians, universally fails of attaining that end; nor is this to be wondered at, as every regulation brought forward with this avowed intention is always so contrived, as to contribute not to the advantage of the oppressed Indian, but solely to that of the person exercising the chief authority.

CHAPTER XVII.

ANNO DOM. 1635.

The Administration of Don Sebastian Corcuera.

On the 25th of June, 1635, Don Sebastian Hurtado de Corcuera, who had been Governor of Panama, took possession of this government, and the same day Señor Guerrero took possession of the archbishopric, although the bulls had not yet arrived. Dissensions immediately begun between these two, originating between the Dominicans and bearded friars, respecting the division of their provinces, and on which account his Excellency was determined to be revenged of the Archbishop, the very first opportunity. An occasion very soon presented itself: the

Archbishop having taken a female slave from an artilleryman, because he had an illicit intercourse with her, the artilleryman met her one day in the street, and, for some unknown cause, murdered her, taking refuge in the church of St. Augustine.

The Governor ordered the troops to seize him in the church, without first applying to the friars; they obeyed their orders, seized the criminal, and delivered him up to their commanding officer, who sentenced him to death. The sentence was executed in front of the church of St. Augustine, a place which had never been used for public punishment: the Archbishop attempted to prevent the violation of the church privileges, but his attempt proved ineffectual.

During the disputes between the Governor and the Archbishop, the Moors were ravaging our towns, and for the space of eight months committed horrible atrocities. His Excellency determined to go in person to chastise them. He sailed from Manila with a squadron on the 2d of February, 1637, and having arrived at Lamitan, the residence of Corralat, petty sovereign of Mindanao, he possessed himself of it with ease. Corralat retired to a hill well defended by batteries, and the best troops he had. The Governor attacked him, but after losing many Spaniards, he sounded a retreat. The day following he renewed the attack by a road more accessible, when he possessed himself of the fort, and made great slaughter of the Moors, who threw themselves headlong over the precipice in their confusion. The Governor now retired to Zamboanga, where he received the chief of Buhayen, and those of the island of Basilan, upon both of whom their fears had operated to beg for peace, promising to consider Corralat as a common enemy, and receive Friars into their dominions.

From Zamboanga he passed to Jolo, and sat down before the famous hill fort of the island, and which the Spaniards had never been able to possess themselves of. He found it, however, so well fortified, that after attempting to batter it, he was obliged to have recourse to some other mode of attack. He prepared five mines, and springing them at the time of assault, he blew up part of the works, with fifty men; but the Spaniards advanced so slow, that the Moors had time to recover themselves, and returning to the charge, repulsed them effectually. The next day two more mines were sprung, which did great damage. The Spaniards then advanced rapidly to the remaining fortification, but behind the rampart which had been blown up, contrary to their expectation, they found another work erected, and by which means they were repulsed. The Governor observing the little effect produced by these assaults, determined to surround the hill, though a league in circumference, with a wall and forts, converting the siege into a strict blockade. This measure, however, proved by no means adequate to the end in view, the besieged defending themselves with great resolution, and destroying numbers of the assailants. It was, therefore, resolved to construct a battery on a position completely commanding the hill. The Moors on this were desirous of capitulating, but the Governor commanded them to surrender at discretion. Thinking these terms harsh, they became desperate, and assaulted the Spanish camp; but not being able to force it, they took the opportunity of quitting the hill by the back part of it, which had been left for the time lightly guarded.

His Excellency found himself in possession of the enemies position, and all their riches, with the Queen and her nephew, Tancun. The Queen requested permission to bring the King and his chiefs into the presence of the Governor; he consented, and she took that opportunity of escaping. The Governor then sent Tancun for the same purpose, and he returned with the keys of the royal coffers; but by the carelessness of the guard, being left too much at liberty, he contrived to get possession of all the treasure, with which he secured his retreat. His Excellency leaving a garrison of two hundred Spaniards, and two hundred Pampangos in Jolo, returned to Manila, where he was received with great honours, as conqueror of Jolo and Mindanao. It is undeniable that Señor Corcuera reduced the inhabitants of Jolo and Mindanao, and would have retained his conquest, had greater harmony subsisted between the Jesuits, and the commanders of the different garrisons. He was successful as a soldier, but unfortunate in his choice of the means to secure his acquisition. The dissensions between the Jesuits and the military rose to such a pitch, that at last all the positions were abandoned, and all our exertions, and sacrifices of men and resources, rendered of no avail.

By the year 1639, the number of Chinese in these islands had increased to thirty thousand, most of them cultivators in Calamba and in Biñan. Among these began a disaffection, which spreading to those of Santa Cruz, Parian, and Manila, they at last converted the church of St. Peter Macati into a kind of strong hold, in which they established their head-quarters. The Governor sent against them two hundred Spaniards, and a large body of Indians, who easily dislodged them from this position. Dispersed into separate bands, they plundered the houses of the Spaniards, and some Indian towns, committing great atrocities. The Spaniards followed them, making dreadful havock among them, from November 1639, to March following, when being reduced in number to seven thousand, they surrendered. Very few of our people were killed, but Manila was reduced to great distress, by the loss of so many of its useful class of citizens, as unquestionably the Chinese were. The Indians fortunately had remained perfectly tranquil, which was rather to be attributed to their fixed hatred of the Chinese, than their attachment to the Spaniards.

In the year 1642, the Archbishop Guerreo visited his diocese, and in the harbour of Naryan, in Mindoro, a pirate seized his vessel, with all his equipage, he himself, with great difficulty, saving himself by flight. This disaster had such an effect upon him, that he died on the 2d of July at Manila, and was buried in the church of St. Augustine.

The kingdom of Portugal, which had been united to the crown of Castile in 1640, shook off the Spanish yoke, and electing the Duke of Braganza King, the possessions of that nation in India immediately followed the example of the mother country, and declared for that family. This year the Dutch reduced Malacca, and by this conquest, and the separation of the Spanish and Portuguese interest, it was apprehended they would renew their attempts on the Philippines, which had now, for many years, remained unmolested by them. This conjecture proved true; they commenced their operations by stationing, for two successive years, a squadron in the route of the ships from Acapulco, but the Jesuits, in the island of Samar, frustrated their design. They then planned the capture of the island of Formosa, with a view to interrupt the commerce to China, and as a ladder for the conquest of the Philippines. They proceeded on the enterprize in the year 1642, with four ships, a patache, and several smaller vessels, and in a few days succeeded in their object, the island having surrendered. Great consternation prevailed

T 2

at Manila on information of this conquest, as it was expected that the Dutch would follow up their success by an attack on that capital; but the glory of repelling these intruders was reserved for the successor of Señor Corcuera.

CHAPTER XVIII.

ANNO DOM. 1644.

The Administration of Don Diego Faxardo.

Don Diego Faxardo, Knight of the order of Santiago, took possession of his government on the 11th of August, 1644, and immediately gave proof of his unrelenting disposition by his conduct towards Señor Corcuera, by confining him in the fort of Santiago, in which he remained five years.

The new Governor found these islands infested by Dutch squadrons, and to enable himself to meet them with effect, he deemed it necessary to unite the whole of the Spanish force, dispersed through the different garrisons. He directed the officer in command at Zamboanga, to enter into an amicable arrangement with Corralat, King of Mindanao, which was effected very satisfactorily, through the mediation of a friar. He likewise directed the officer commanding at Jolo to adopt similar measures with the King of that island, and evacuating all the forts, to bring all the Spaniards to Manila; but this was not to be effected so easily, Salicala, hereditary Prince of the kingdom, having gone to Batavia, soliciting assistance from the Dutch, to drive the Spaniards from the island. They, however, spared him only two ships, with which trifling aid, having made many attempts against our principal position, which was defended vigorously by Don Estevan Ugalde, a valiant Biscayan, the Dutch retired to Batavia, promising the Moors to return next year, with a more effective force. The Jesuit friar was, in the mean time, commissioned to make peace with them, which he effected on very advantageous terms. Jolo being thus evacuated, the Dutch arrived at the appointed time with the promised assistance; and finding that the Spaniards had retired to Zamboanga, they determined on attempting the capture of the fort of Caldera, in Mindanao, but they were repulsed with such loss, that they made a rapid retreat to Batavia.

The following year, the Dutch again appeared in these seas, with a squadron of twelve ships, when eleven of them remaining on the coast of Batan, the commodore came forward alone, to reconnoitre Cavite. Señor Corcuera, who was in confinement in the fort, as already mentioned, immediately saw the error the Dutch commander had committed, in not making the attack with his whole force, while the place was in an unguarded and defenceless state. Every advantage was taken of the error, and Cavite was furnished, without delay, with the necessary reinforcements, and supplies of ammunition and provisions. On the third day the Dutch squadron made their attack, but the Governor, Andras Azaldegui, a very active man, defended the place so effectually, that great slaughter ensued, and the Dutch General received a wound, of which he died. On this they retired, and disembarked in Pampanga, where the Alcalde Mayor of the province having collected six hundred Pampangos, and fortified himself as well as possible in the convent of Abucay, the Dutch assaulted him, when the Indians fled in such disorder, and with such precipitation, that four hundred of them were killed in the pursuit. The Dutch not deeming it prudent to remove far from their ships, returned on board, and disembarked a second time in the town of Samal, where the Spaniards having gone to Manila, the Indians alone remained, who repulsed them, and compelled them to take refuge in their ships.

They then took their station close to

Mareveles, to intercept our commerce, and while here they had information that a galleon, built at Leyte, was on her way to Manila. They despatched six ships to take her, but the commander understanding that the Dutch were in these seas, put into a harbour, and fortifying the entrance with batteries, remained perfectly secure from all insult, and the Dutch deeming the attempt unjustifiable, returned to Batavia, without reaping any advantage from their expedition. .

Salicala, son of the King of Jolo, a turbulent character, notwithstanding the peace he had concluded with the Spaniards, begun to infest our seas with a squadron, which committed great depredations in every quarter; and Cachile, Lord of Tup Tup, in Borneo, having followed his example, it was found necessary to send against them an adequate force. The Spaniards encountered the squadron of Cachile between Masbate and Burias, and an engagement took place, in which he was killed, and his fleet dispersed. Immediately on this Salicala retired to Jolo, where his attention became sufficiently occupied, in disputes respecting the succession to the throne. The Moors of Borneo, imitating the conduct of the Indians of Jolo in their piracies, the Governor sent Major Monforte with orders to chastise them severely, as a warning to the rest. Monforte landed in Borneo, burning and destroying all the towns within his reach, together with great quantities of provisions, and a number of vessels, and making about two hundred prisoners, thus retaliating on them for their piratical attacks on us. Exclusive of these continual depredations of the Moors and Dutch, the provinces in Luzon were by no means in a tranquil state.

A commotion, likewise, was begun in Palapag, by murdering the Jesuit friar, who was the curate of the place; and, to enhance the criminality of the action, and comprehend every one in the rebellion, Sumoroy, who was the assassin, was for two days parading the town, avowing publicly that he killed the friar; and, setting at liberty two insurgents, whom the Jesuits had confined, he ordered the people to plunder the church and convent: from this source, the insurrection spread through the whole island. The Camarines imitated the conduct of the people of Palapag, in every thing but the murder of the friars. The island of Zebu, likewise, notwithstanding its garrison, wavered in its loyalty; and, indeed, all the islands were ripe for rebellion: the people of Caraga, however, were the most violent, having murdered many Spaniards and Friars. There is no question that the Bisayas would have been lost on this occasion, had not a stop been put to these atrocities in due time.

The Governor sent a force to Palapag, and ordered that four hundred Indians of

Lutao, who had been lately converted from Mahometanism, should be incorporated with this force sent from Manila, and jointly attack the rebels. The Jesuit friar, Vincente Damian, took compassion on the misguided Indians, and attempted to persuade them to return to their obedience; but, thinking themselves strong enough to overcome the Spaniards, they would not listen to reason, and fortified themselves on a hill, which Sumoroy had made his head quarters. Captain Roxas commanded the Spaniards, Don Andres Azaldeguy, who was the proper commanding officer, having had orders from the government, to go and secure the property, in a ship which had been lost on the coast of Camarines. Roxas was a man of ability and bravery, and came to the resolution of assaulting the hill in the night, when the rebels would be less on their guard. The Spaniards arrived at the outposts, when they were discovered, and notice given to Sumoroy. The precipitation with which the Indians fled is incredible: it resembled that of a flock of goats, our people following them, and making great slaughter. Sumoroy attempted to escape; but his people killed him, with the view of ingratiating themselves with the Spaniards, and delivered up his head to Roxas, who placed it on a pole as a warning to the rest. The friars being now able to return to their duty, in the respective towns, soon reduced the discontented to obedience.

The ringleader of the rebellion in Caraga was an Indian, named Dabao, who was not in the least suspected of disaffection. He entered one day into the fort, bringing with him eight men with their hands bound, apparently with the view of surrendering them; but yet, at the same time, so loosely bound, as to escape when they chose. When the Spanish officer came out to receive them, Dabao struck him on the head with his sword, and the eight men, immediately releasing themselves, unexpectedly attacked the people in the fort. They made such carnage, that only one friar and five soldiers escaped, by throwing themselves from the wall, and retiring to the convent, where they fortified themselves. The Indians immediately forsook the town and fled to the mountains, when the friar, and the Spaniards who were in the convent, built a boat, and retired along the coast to another town, to which the insurrection had not spread.

The Governor sent them relief from Manila, and offered a pardon to those who should return to their towns, and their allegiance as before. The Spaniards, however, broke their word, and hanged many of the ringleaders.

On the day of Saint Andrew, which was the anniversary of the victory the Spaniards obtained over Limahon, about eight o'clock at night, an earthquake happened, which destroyed almost all Manila, with the exception of the church and convent of St. Augustine. The public edifices, in particular, were nearly all thrown down and destroyed, and more than six hundred people buried in the ruins: some were found alive between the stones and the wood, who had remained there even three days. The calamity reached the towns of the islands; in Cagayan, a hill was rased from its foundation, and fell on a town, burying in its fall all the inhabitants. In some parts the earth sunk; and, in others, torrents of sand burst out, overwhelming man and beast. Many other extraordinary changes occurred in the course of sixty days, during which a succession of earthquakes prevailed. The people of Manila left the city to live in huts in the fields, until it was ascertained that they might return in safety to their houses. It was said that the image of St. Francis, placed in the house of an Indian of Dilao, sweated most copiously during this calamity, and shed abundance of tears; in consequence, he was elected patron of earthquakes, and is designated St. Francis of Tears.

As a proof of that harshness which characterized Señor Faxardo, it will be sufficient to mention his conduct to Christoval Romero, whom the Viceroy of Mexico had sent, to bring him intelligence of the state of these islands, two years having elapsed without the usual ship having appeared at Acapulco. He arrived at the port of Lampon, and, understanding that the Dutch were infesting these seas, he landed the silver, and despatched it to Manila, in order that he might with less risk get round. Soon after he had sent away the silver, the Dutch arrived, and entered the port with their launches. Romero being far inferior in force to the enemy, burnt his vessel, as he saw no chance of saving it, and came to Manila by land. Every body considered this man as entitled to great praise for his conduct on the occasion, and expected that he would be well received and rewarded; but the rigorous Governor, on the plea that the burning of the launch was an act of cowardice, imprisoned him, and condemned him to lose his head. All Manila clamoured against this sentence; and the object of it appealed to the Royal Audience, who revoked it. This rigour of the Governor was imputed to his not having been duly bribed by Romero; but nothing of that nature could be absolutely proved against him.

About this time, the hospital or college of St. Juan de Letran was founded by Juan Geronimo Romero, who compassionating the situation of unfortunate orphans, took them into his house, and carefully brought them up. His Majesty being informed of this praise-worthy conduct, by a royal order protected the establishment; but granted so little in aid of it, that recourse was necessarily had to the contributions of the well disposed, in order to render it of more general use. It was, at length, removed to a spot behind the city: the boys were allowed a blue coat, cap, &c., and were supported, as in others, with the additional aid of a college pension, to enable them to pursue their studies at the university; the college having no establishment of this nature.

CHAPTER XIX.

ANNO DOM. 1653.

The Administration of Don Sabiniano Manrique de Lara.

The ship San Francisco Xavier arrived in Cavite in July, 1653, bringing the new Governor, Don Sabiniano Manrique de Lara; the Archbishop of Manila, Don Miguel Poblete; the Bishop of Ylocos, Don Rodrigo de Cordinas, a Dominican; and the Oidor, Don Juan Bolivar. The Governor immediately, as was usual, sat in judgment on his predecessor, who, apprehensive that he might be deprived of his liberty, retired into the college of Jesuits, securing his personal safety in this sacred asylum. The Archbishop fixed the month of March for a jubilee, on which occasion an immense concourse of people assembled, and he, with great solemnity, invoked the blessing of the Almighty on these islands.

Many calamities occurred during this administration, such as the small-pox, famine, and a dreadful earthquake, which ruined many edifices, and did much injury; but what affected the Governor much more than all these, was the revolt of the Indians and Chinese, and the ravages committed by the Moors of Mindanao. The Spaniards were at peace with Corrolat, King of Mindanao, and he appeared perfectly satisfied; but the chief men, turbulent and warlike, urged him to break it.

The Governor sent two Jesuits and some Spaniards, in the nature of an embassy, to strengthen our existing amity with the King: when, without any respect for their characters as ambassadors, and, listening to the representations of his nephew

Balatamay, he murdered them all, and excused his atrocity to the Governor of Zamboanga, throwing the blame on his nephew, whom, he alleged, he could not punish, on account of his great power in the state.

In the letter which he wrote to the Governor of Manila, he laid the blame on the Jesuit, who was at the head of the embassy; thus indicating his intention, by these contradictory falsehoods, of gaining time to draw to his party the King of Jolo, and other chiefs of the Moluccas.

Don Francisco Esteyvar, who was Governor of Zamboanga, despatched against him an armament of ten carracoas, whose rowers were Indians of Lutao, and who, though they had been converted to Christianity, felt for Corrolat as a countryman. Nothing could persuade them to row against the Moors, excusing themselves under various pretexts; and, although they could have been compelled, yet Don

Fernando Bobadilla, who commanded the expedition, fearing that they would desert him in the time he most wanted them, and not desirous of exposing himself to such a risk, returned to Zamboanga.

As the Spaniards had delayed the chastisement of the Moors for the murder of their ambassadors, they were induced, as might be expected, to commit still greater ravages than those they had yet been guilty of, and Don Sabiniano de Lara sent against them a considerable squadron, under the command of a man, valiant in the cabinet, but who proved the reverse in the field. He repeatedly showed a disposition to attack the Moors; but, on various pretexts, avoided coming to an engagement, and at last retired to Zebu, abandoning the cause, and leaving the Moors to return quietly to their own country. The Governor of Zamboanga, however, acting a different part, and determined to chastise the Moors, collected some vessels, and retaliated on their country, the ravages they had committed on ours.

A slight disturbance, about this time, took place in the province of Pampanga, the cause of which was as follows: the late Governor having ordered a ship to be built in Camboxa, sent all the necessary workmen in a vessel, which he patched up, and launched for the purpose. After having completed their work, and when they were on their return from Camboxa to Manila, they encountered a storm, so violent, that the vessel was wrecked, and almost all the people perished. The galleon, San Francisco Xavier, was lost in the same storm on the coast of Samar, and two other ships which were going to Acapulco were forced back. The galleon, La Concepcion, too, was so unfortunate as to be driven back twice, having suffered severely in her rigging. To repair these losses, it was necessary that a greater quantity of wood should be cut than was customary, and that with unusual expedition. The Indians suffered always severely in these undertakings, as they were obliged to leave their towns for the mountains, where, their wages being very small, and their treatment very bad, they too often fell a sacrifice to sickness. The overseer of the present wood cutting was a man of great severity, and, as the wood was to be cut with all despatch, he had recourse, with the poor Indians, to measures which humanity could not justify, in order to expedite the work. Resisting this oppressive conduct, they mutinied, and the mutiny extended through all the towns, although they did not behave with disrespect to the church or friars. To quell this sedition before it took a wider range, the Governor took up his residence in Macabebe, which is the first town in the province, from Manila, taking with him some troops, and ordering into his presence some of the ringleaders. The Indians, naturally timid, had already repented of this disturbance, when the friars interfering, it was completely quelled, and the principal ringleader, an Indian named Maniago, was conveyed to Manila, being considered as too dangerous an inhabitant of the province.

The bad example of those in Pampanga, induced the Indians of Pangasinan to rebel, electing as their King an Indian, called Marlong. They murdered the Alcalde Mayor of the province, with all his family, and, upon this being known in Manila, the Governor sent troops by sea and land to quell the sedition; but the Dominican friars possessed such power over the Indians, that they were restored to their duty without firing one gun; and their King, Marlong, was delivered up and hanged immediately.

When the Indians of Pangasinan began their rebellion, they had sent emissaries to the provinces of Cagayan, Ylocos, and

Zambales. In this last they made little progress, but in Ylocos, an Indian called Manzano, headed the rebellion, and, having collected a number of malcontents, he attacked the Spaniards, murdered the Friar Bacarra, and ill treated the Bishop Cardinas, on which the Alcalde Mayor and some friars fled to Manila; but the province of Pangasinan being by this time reduced to subjection, the troops were sent against Manzano, and soon reduced him likewise; and the ringleaders of both were executed.

The civil wars of China were the cause of the conquest of that country by the Tartars. A Chinese named Ly, having urged the provinces remote from the court to revolt, and meeting with no opposition, arrived at the capital (Pekin), on which occasion, either from treason or cowardice, all abandoned the Emperor, who, seeing himself thus forsaken, cut off, according to their usual custom, the head of his daughter, that she might not fall into the hands of the rebels, and afterwards hanged himself on a tree, to avoid a similar disgrace.

All acknowledged the authority of Ly, except the army, which had been opposed to the Tartars, and which, fearing the result of this rebellion, made peace with them, and they united against the common enemy, Ly, whom they soon drove from Pekin. Nothing more was ever heard of this rebellion; but, the Tartars having by this means got into the interior of China, though they met with some opposition, yet, finally, they reduced the whole of the empire, and it continues still under the Tartar dynasty.

A poor Chinese, who had fled from Macao to Manila, where he was baptized by the name of Nicolas, and where he became a shop-keeper, afterwards went to Japan, where he married; but finding that he did not acquire riches quick enough, he entered the Chinese army, where he rose very high, being appointed General against the rebels. Zunchin, who was the last Emperor of the Chinese race, having hanged himself, as already noticed, Nicolas sided with the Tartars, by whom he was apparently well received. The Tartar Emperor heaped favours upon him, and named him as one of his tributary monarchs, under the title of Pignan, which signifies, conqueror of the south. By these means he lulled him into security; and having at last imprisoned him and all his family, completed his treachery by blowing him, and the greater part of them, up with gunpowder.

His son, Cogseng, after this disgraceful transaction, turned pirate, and sufficiently revenged the death of his father by ravaging the Chinese coasts and islands. He was the conqueror of the island of Formosa, and the first who triumphed over the arms of Europeans. The Dutch, at this time, were complete masters of the island, they possessed two thousand Europeans, with sufficient artillery and ships; when hearing that the Chinese intended to attack them, they united all their forces in Tayguan; but the pirate, who came with about one hundred thousand men, landed on the opposite coast of the island, and immediately entered on the cultivation of the soil. A short time after, he invested the fort of Tayguan, and the Dutch capitulated, after a seven months siege, by which they were allowed to leave the island, with the ships they had in the port.

Cogseng, elated with this success, determined to become master of the Philippines, for which purpose he sent the Friar Victorio Riccio, a Dominican, with the title of his Ambassador, to Manila, with a letter to the Governor, in which he required him to recognize him as Sovereign, and pay him tribute, threatening, if he refused, to ravage his coasts with his fleet. On the 18th of May, 1662, the friar arrived on this embassy at Manila, and delivered his letter with great secrecy, which, however, was not long withheld from the public. The Governor without delay began to levy troops, repair the fortifications, and recal all the forces to the capital; and in order to be as secure as possible, he sent away all the Chinese merchants, and others that were established in the islands. Upon this being known, it was whispered that the Governor intended to decapitate all the Chinese, who, being naturally cowards, believed the knife already at their throats, and retired to the mountains, from whence some passed, with great risk, in small boats to Formosa. The day on which the Governor called the Chinese chiefs before him, in order to intimate to them that they must retire, the remaining Chinese believing that they were all to be murdered, took up arms; but the Dominicans had sufficient influence to prevail on them to remain quiet. The Governor now sent back Friar Riccio to Cogseng with an answer to his letter, but, on Riccio's arrival, he found the pirate dead of a fever, Manila being by this means released from the danger with which she was threatened. The Chinese who had fled to Formosa, circulated a thousand calumnies, which would have cost Friar Riccio his life, if he had not been saved by the son of Cogseng, who had succeeded his father in power; but not possessing the warlike spirit of his father, he sent an Ambassador to Manila, to make a treaty of amity and commerce with the Spaniards. Although the expedition of Cogseng had not reached Manila, the place of its destination, the effects of it had fallen very heavy on the islands, as all the churches and convents near Manila were destroyed, to prevent the enemy from converting them into military stations.

The Governor of Ternate had abandoned that station, by no means easy to be recovered, as the garrison was, in its retreat to Manila, accompanied by the Indians, called Mahhicas, who were the best friends to the Spanish cause, and who were then settled at the mouth of the river Marigondon, where their descendants remain to this hour. The garrisons too of Calamianes and Zamboanga evacuated these stations; and as they had always been a check on the Moors of Jolo and Mindanao, opportunities were by this means offered of committing with impunity such ravages in the Bisayas, that the friars were compelled to abandon the province of Calamianes.

Don Sabiniano Manrique de Lara had governed these islands with great prudence, but notwithstanding this, several articles of impeachment were preferred against him, and he was fined seventy thousand dollars. On appealing, however, to the council of the Indies, the sentence was reversed, and the fine remitted; but disgusted with the world, he retired to Malaga, his native country, and took the monastic habit.

CHAPTER XX.

ANNO DOM. 1663.

The Administration of Don Diego Salcedo.

Don Diego de Salcedo not being able, by the prevalence of the south-west monsoon, to reach Manila by the ordinary route of the straits of Bernardino, he made Cagayan, where he landed, and travelled across the island to the city, and took possession of his government in September, 1663. Immediately on his arrival, he held out every encouragement to commerce, and preparation was made for sending the usual ship to Acapulco as early in the season as possible, in order to avoid those misfortunes which had too frequently taken place.

This conduct of the Governor at first gave great satisfaction to the merchants of Manila; but they began very soon to discover his diligence was directed only to his own individual benefit, or that of his friends, as due care had been taken by them to buy up all the best goods, leaving in the market only those of inferior quality; and that no opportunity might be afforded to the merchants to procure a fresh supply of the different articles from the coast, he despatched the ship before the coasters could possibly arrive. By this means almost all the commerce of Acapulco, for that season, centered in him and his friends. About this time the news arrived of the death of Philip the Fourth, and the Archbishop was attacked with protracted illness, which ended in extreme debility, of which he died, 1667. The attention of Salcedo had been completely occupied by the violent disputes, which, during the whole period of his government, subsisted between him and the ecclesiastical authorities, and which terminated in the Commissary of the Inquisition of Mexico ordering him to be seized, and conveyed on board the patache destined for Acapulco, in which ship he died, 1669.

END OF VOL. I.

T. DAVISON, Lombard-street,
Whitefriars, London.

Zeitfracht Medien GmbH
Ferdinand-Jühlke-Straße 7
99095 Erfurt, Deutschland
produktsicherheit@kolibri360.de